Ballrooms and Ugly Poodles
Semi-Tall Tales of a Palm Beach Waitress

Ballrooms and Ugly Poodles
Semi-Tall Tales of a Palm Beach Waitress

Katie Schnack

This is a work of fiction. Names, characters, places and incidents are either a product of the author's imagination or are used fictitiously. Any resemblance to any persons, living or dead, business establishments, events or locals is entirely coincidental.

Ballrooms and Ugly Poodles: Semi-Tall Tales of a Palm Beach Waitress

Published by Cotton Publishing
Copyright © by Katie Schnack
Cover art by Allison Bright

First edition: January, 2013

For Jenna in Heaven and Kyle on Earth

CONTENTS

Acknowledgements

So many amazing people had a hand in making this book possible, and I am grateful for each and every one of them. Thank you Allison Bright for your beautiful cover design and generosity. Christy McFerren, thank you for your website design, coding skills and friendship. Thank you Mallory Molitor, Katie Radzik and Samantha Robey for your editing work- your time and care is so appreciated. Thank you to the amazing team at Shelton Interactive for all your wisdom, support and friendship. Thank you to my amazing family and friends for not calling me crazy (to my face) when I said I wanted to be a writer. Thank you to the people of Palm Beach for giving me such great material to write about. And to my amazing husband Kyle - your love, creative genius and encouragement is invaluable. Thank for making me laugh every single day. And to God – thank you for creating such a crazy world full of amazing stories, and giving me the ability to tell them. To Him be the glory.

The mundane is often contrived, but the ridiculous is often Palm Beach.

-Col. Trent Stephens

A note from the author

You may be wondering who Col. Trent Stephens is, who I quoted on the previous page. He is a lovely friend of mine – "colonel" is a real legal title awarded to him by the Commonwealth of Kentucky, and it makes him sound important and fancy. However, my husband is also an official Kentucky colonel and he has never been to Kentucky and doesn't eat fried chicken so… go figure.

Anyway, Col. Stephens spit this quote out late one night as we were sipping on $3 Walmart wine and tie-dying t-shirts, (a typical Saturday night for us), and I thought it was the perfect way to start out this book. I continued to feel that way the next day when the fog of cheap booze and fabric-dye fumes subsided, so voila – it made it into print. Please note that all names, places and scenarios in *Ballrooms and Ugly Poodles* are either a product of my imagination or are used fictitiously.

That being said, I really did work at a fancy Palm Beach hotel during college. These stories are loosely based off of that amazing opportunity. So as you read, remember that the crazier the scenario, the more likely it was something I actually experienced. Because as Col. Stephens so eloquently stated – it is easy to make-up the ordinary, but the extraordinary comes from the real, extravagant and crazy world known as Palm Beach, Florida.

-Katie Schnack

Ballrooms and Ugly Poodles
Semi-Tall Tales of a Palm Beach Waitress

Looking Hot In a Tuxedo Takes Skill

My name is Katie and let me assure you, I am a female. I can prove it to you but I have my dignity. That is why my head slightly tilted in confusion when I was handed a man's tuxedo. I was in the uniform room of my new job. The air was filled with an odd scent, something that could be best described as a mix of pickles and laundry detergent. A scratchy Spanish radio station played quietly, and one of the overhead florescent lights was blinking. Two men were arguing loudly outside the door in Creole, and the air conditioner must have been broken, because a bead of sweat formed on my upper lip.

"I'm sorry, but can I get the ladies uniform?" I asked the woman who was helping me, already suspecting what the answer would be but not wanting to accept my fate of having to wear such a terrible ensemble. She didn't look up from the dirty shirts dotted with mystery stains that she was sorting through as she mumbled, "Honey, there ain't no 'ladies uniform,' they are all the same."

I stared blankly at the black polyester pants that were baggy at the thigh yet tight at the ankle, the stiff white button-up shirt that smelled of starch and body odor, and the thick three-button suit coat. Don't forget the silky black tie.

In the changing room, I slipped the pants over my tan legs. When I pulled them up, I realized the waist sat much higher than my belly button, and the hem fell just above my ankles. They reminded me of the ugly tweed suit pants my Aunt Karen wore in the 90's when she rushed off to her accounting job at the Bark and Purr Pet Center. I fumbled with the necktie, trying to remember what my dad looked like as he dressed for work. I gave up after two unsuccessful tuck and pulls.

Just when I thought every possible inch of my skin had been covered, I emerged from the dressing room and the uniform lady handed me white cotton serving gloves. "Don't forget these, sugar," she said. She looked at me as if she would rather be at home watching reruns of *Oprah*. I looked at her as though she had just handed me a pile of dog poop. White gloves? What, do I have a sun allergy? The only part of my flesh that would see the light of day in this uniform was my freckled face, which, after five minutes in this astronaut suit, would be makeup-less and shiny from sweating in the South Florida heat.

I finally managed to maneuver the necktie into something that resembled the proper knot, and I buttoned up the fat padded buttons on the front of my jacket. I reached into the pocket and my fingers burst through a small hole. Awesome. And by awesome, I mean disgusting. But then, I felt a small mass shoved somewhere towards the bottom of the coat, and I became slightly intrigued. I immediately had optimistic thoughts. Perhaps it was a long forgotten wad of cash from the previous owner, just waiting for me to discover it? Perhaps this was the world's way of rewarding me for having to wear such an ugly uniform. I tend to be far too optimistic for my own good sometimes.

I traversed my fingers into the twilight zone between jacket and lining, my bravery stemming from the hopes of a few extra dollars. I scrunched my eyes closed and said a silent prayer as I pulled the mass from its fabric grave, hoping the cash would be enough to support my Dunkin Doughnuts coffee addiction for the week. I opened my eyes, and instead of George Washington and his friends sitting in my gloved hand, it was a tampon. Yes, a tampon. Nothing gets you more excited about showing up at work than discovering someone else's feminine product in your jacket. Let's get this party started.

You may be wondering why I would take a job if I detested the uniform so strongly. The reason is the same as for most other obnoxious situations in life – money. I needed it. It was the beginning of my sophomore year of college, and my bank account had less meat in it than a vegan's refrigerator. Freshman year I lived happily ignorant of financial responsibility, surviving off of cafeteria food and a small amount of money I had saved from my job at a dilapidated mini-golf course the previous summer. It is worth noting one of my main tasks at this putt-putt land from hell was spraying bird poop off a giant cement T-rex statue every morning. Professional dinosaur bather – the best line on my resume thus far. But then, sophomore year rolled around, my school meal plan decreased, and the harsh reality hit that if I wanted to buy textbooks *and* support my clearance rack shopping habit, I would have to get a job. Thus, the search for employment began.

Soon after I accepted my fate of having to actually work for a living, my college held a job fair outside the cafeteria, so I went to investigate. As I meandered through the different booths, I was beyond unenthusiastic about the choices presented before me. Option 1: Being a chicken slinger at Chick Fil-A. Hmm… coming home every night smelling like French fries, my hair crusty from strawberry milkshake backsplash? No thanks.

Option 2: The school library. Getting paid way too little for putting books on shelves, and having to shush my peers every five minutes, when I am easily one of the loudest, most talkative people you will ever meet… no thank you.

Option 3: Banquet server in Palm Beach. Intriguing. At this booth was a man over six feet tall with dark hair, olive skin and a serious face. He had a little gold plated nametag pinned to his green shirt that read 'Robert.' I was captivated by that gold nametag as it glistened in the sun. I wanted that gold nametag, I wanted it.

Robert was at the job fair representing a historic, five diamond hotel that sat right on the beach. They were looking for banquet servers, no experience needed. This was good, as my resume at that point was beyond pitiful. My painful memories of T-rex washing become overshadowed by daydreams of working on the island as a Palm Beach waitress, smiling as I gracefully served fruity mixed drinks poolside. The guests would be friendly, tipping me generously before offering to take me out on their yacht later that evening. Yes, this sounded much better than the mini-golf course.

"Hey, how's it going?" I said, as I looked into the eyes of this dark, serious looking man and immediately felt intimidated. He did not smile. "Are you interested in the banquet serving position?" he asked.

"Do you get to wear a gold name tag?"

"Yes."

"Then I am interested." Robert handed me a piece of off-white paper with the hotel's name elegantly printed across the top in dark green script. Someone who deemed it necessary to use extremely large, pretentious words, had written out a description of the job. I skimmed through it, and decided the job did not seem too bad. Basically I would be serving pre-ordered dinners at parties held on the hotel grounds. I then got to the part where it said how much the position paid, and I almost dropped my algebra book on the sidewalk. That was okay with me because I hated math and believed it should be banned from every institution of higher learning and replaced with a course on how to draw pictures of kittens wearing top hats.

"Wow, ah… Robert, this job pays very well," I said, while trying to disguise the look of shock on my face.

"Well, we are a prestigious establishment and we expect the very best from our staff," he explained, then glanced down at his perfectly manicured nails and sniffed the air loudly into his large, hair filled nostrils. "And besides, it's Palm Beach. That is practically standard pay for serving."

I smiled at him, hoping no food was stuck in my teeth from lunch. I thanked him, then shook his hand firmly like I learned in business class and walked briskly back to my dorm, the thoughts of my bank account being filled with money putting a little spring in my step. Two days later I was called in for an interview, and as simple as that I became a banquet server at one of the most luxurious hotels in the country.

My then boyfriend Kyle was also hired. Little did we know this job would pay for an engagement ring and honeymoon a mere two years later. Wait: pause for a second. This is probably the point where you are thinking 'She got married before she even finished COLLEGE?' Congratulations, you are the 931st person to be shocked by this fact. How original. Yes, I was a youthful, wedded collegiate. Yes, I am 'that girl' who tied the knot unusually young. Listen up you little judger - Kyle and I met when we were twelve at a birthday party in Minnesota, where we both grew up a mile apart from each other. I was all hopped up on Mountain Dew and he had so much gel in his hair it look like he stuck his head in a doughnut glazing machine. We started dating a week later – whatever dating even looks like at age twelve, anyway. I never got sick of him; he never got sick of me, and BAM! Married at age twenty-one and we still are obsessed with each other. Pardon the cheesiness. Let's move on.

When Kyle and I showed up to get our 'new employee tour' of the hotel, I quickly realized I was stepping into a world far foreign to my Midwestern mentality. Our new supervisor Craig met us at the front door. Craig was an Indian man about five and half feet tall with a big smile, one missing tooth, and as I would soon learn - no concept of personal space or breath mints.

"Welcome to your new place of employment," Craig said, gesturing dramatically toward the heavy wooden doors. A couple of valets nearby were leaning against the wall, looking at us placidly, all their energy drained from chasing after BMW's all day. As we entered the hotel, the air escaped my lungs as I gawked at the architectural beauty before me. The high vaulted ceilings towered overhead, the Florida afternoon sun glinting off the shiny gold leaf covering. The carpet felt plush under my feet, and not a speck of dirt was visible on the perfectly vacuumed floor. Fresh red apples sat in a wire bowl at the front desk, their warmth contrasting against the cool shade of the marble walls. A massive chandelier hung in the middle of the lobby, dripping with thousands of antique crystals, each one standing as a symbol of wealth and beauty.

Craig began the tour by showing us a portrait of the man who built the hotel back in the 1800's – a railroad tycoon with a dangerously funky moustache. I love mustaches for their ridiculousness, but hate them at the same time. I am sure you can understand. My friend's father has a moustache so large it looked like a cat died under his nose. We were eating sandwiches together once, and I stared at him across the table in disgust as large clumps of mayonnaise got stuck in the wiry hairs. I wanted to throw my plate at his head and scream at him to shave that ungodly beast from his face. But instead, I stayed silent and vowed never to eat mayo again. That is probably why I hate mustaches. And mayonnaise. Anyway, back to the hotel.

The building burned down several times in its history before it was rebuilt to be the grandeur it is now. Some say the railroad tycoon set the fires to collect insurance money and rebuild it bigger and better. I would believe it - you can't trust a man with such an extravagant cluster of hair above his lip. He can hide things in it, like weapons, stolen children, and rotten mayonnaise clumps. But the burning and rebuilding may have been worth it, because what stands now is a beautiful hotel that instantly transports me to a more privileged world, one without student loans, car payments, and unpaid medical bills.

The hotel has three massive ballrooms that look like they came straight out of a fairy tale. Two sit side-by-side, equal but unique in their beauty. One has puffy white clouds painted on the ceiling and a huge crystal chandelier hanging in the center. The room next to it is right along the ocean, its floor-to-ceiling windows giving a perfect view of the Atlantic, which at night is illuminated by underwater lights. On the other side of the building is a huge circular room with an elaborate and breathtaking mural painted on the ceiling. It looks as if Michelangelo himself had taken a Palm Beach vacation, and spent most of it painting this ballroom, perhaps sipping a piña colada as he worked.

There are two smaller rooms where many wedding ceremonies take place. One is blinding as you enter it, as its ceiling is covered with real gold cherub heads that gleam in the light. Personally, the hundreds of baby faces freak me out, and I would not want them witnessing my holy matrimony, but to each his own. The other small ballroom has a border near the ceiling made up of paintings of important historical figures like George Washington and Sacagawea. One of the portraits is just of the back of a guy's head. What the heck? Who painted that? Who is that backwards man? I will never know. So annoying.

Several floors of guest rooms are piled on top of the main level. On the highest floor sits two massive suites with perfect views of the ocean, each containing their own dining room more luxurious than one I will ever own. In the bathrooms, if you press a button a mini television appears in the glass of the mirror, so you can hang out with Wolf Blitzer as you get ready for your evening affair. Hello Mr. Blitzer, I don't know why you are in my bathroom, but I like it.

The entire building wraps around a courtyard, with four elaborate staircases leading down to an uneven floor of ancient cobblestone. A fountain sits in the middle, with four cherub statues each spitting water into a flat pool. Try to have some class and avoid staring at their tiny stone-sculpted wieners, please.

I didn't really understand what I was getting myself into until I took that first tour of the hotel. The dimly lit human resource building down the road where I interviewed did not do it justice. I thought this was just going to be another ho-hum job to get me through my younger years. But no, I was about to immerse myself in the lives of the rich and famous, something that didn't happen too often in my hometown of Coon Rapids, Minnesota. (Yes, that really is the name of my city. Google it if you don't believe me.) Furthermore, the HR lady did not inform me when I applied on that steamy September afternoon that I was actually applying to work in a nut house. You see, I was under the impression I would be just passing around champagne, smiling at guests and telling them exactly what they wanted to hear. Nobody told me about the peculiar creatures I would be forced to interact with called 'Palm Beach Socialites.' Nobody told me I would see and hear things I wish I could erase from my memory, but they are burned there like the time I accidentally saw my fat Aunt Bertha naked after her shower. Nobody told me Palm Beach is crazy.

As the tour wrapped up and I recovered from the shock of how beautiful the hotel was, I began getting excited for the waitressing escapades before me. I began daydreaming about how I could meet someone famous, or get tipped $1,000 by a lonely old man – the possibilities were endless. However, none of my Palm Beach shenanigans would happen without my new trusty sidekick, the tuxedo. So, with my body wrapped in black polyester, tie knotted tight and white serving gloves on, I began my adventure as a Palm Beach waitress.

Un-bunch Those Panties Sir; There Are Enough Scallops For Everyone

Like I said, I grew up in Minnesota, more specifically in a suburb of Minneapolis named after raccoons. You know, those nasty creatures that dig through your trash and sometimes attack people's faces with their gnarly claws and spread rabies. It makes sense to name a town after such creatures. Oh wait, no it doesn't.

My childhood was typical of a suburban Midwest upbringing. My parents still live in the house they built before I was born. We have had the same small fishing boat our entire life, ate at the same Burger King every Saturday, and had the same bony orange cat for most of my life, until one day she croaked at the ripe age of eighteen. Our next attempt at cat ownership proved less successful, although more exciting. Theo the cat ran away only a few months after we got him. He hid in a neighbor's shed and froze to death in the forty below weather. My dad, always sentimental when it comes to pets, brought him home to thaw out on our kitchen counter so he could fit him in a box and give him a proper burial. My sister woke up from a nap and stumbled in the kitchen to make some lunch, and I heard her yell, "Dad, can you please take the dead cat off the counter, I want to make a turkey sandwich." As I said, a fairly typical Midwestern upbringing.

As I entered my teen years I was plagued by perpetual dullness. My high school social life consisted of sitting in musty smelling basements while one of my punk rock wannabe friends strummed a guitar and we all pretended to be entertained, when in reality, we were bored out of our minds. That pretty much sums up my experience living in Coon Rapids.

But there is one thing Minnesota is known for, besides the freezing winters, over abundance of lakes, and wide repertoire of casserole recipes – the people are really friendly. They are the type of creatures who like to cook for the Lutheran church potluck, enjoy lazy weekends at the lake, and watch the Vikings play every Sunday under a warm blanket, beer in hand and black lab snoozing at their feet. Because everyone is generally polite, (and have funny Midwest accents that bring joy to your soul), the people of my home state have been dubbed 'Minnesota nice.' But despite these kind-hearted humans of the north, Coon Rapids was too small for my ever-expanding personality. When college came around, I chose a school with more entertainment options besides playing Frisbee golf and learning the art of the keg stand. I wanted sunshine, ocean water and adventure. So, I high-tailed it to South Florida, lost my accent, got a tan, and only looked back at Christmastime.

It only took a few days of working at the hotel for me to realize the people of Palm Beach are far different than the people I grew up around. In the spirit of making up catchy phrases to describe the population of a geographic location, let's call the residents of Palm Beach, 'Palm Beach Ridiculous.' Now I assure you, many people I met from the island are kind, generous creatures. However, several have made me stop and ponder how it is even possible for a person to act the way they do and still associate themselves with the human race. Working in Palm Beach, you are constantly surrounded by people who have everything the world tells them they should have, yet they still seem to be more miserable than a dolphin in a dirty tank at a bankrupt zoo. It reminds me again and again that money really cannot buy happiness, no matter how much you have. However, let's get real: it can buy you smaller thighs and a great purse.

It was my first week at work. I was starting to get the hang of things, and felt confident after the boot camp they made me go through just to serve someone a steak dinner. Training consisted of five days of being yelled at by a veteran server from Egypt who had such a thick accent I couldn't understand a single word he was saying. I eventually just guessed at what to do, and he would yell at me for making a mistake, and then I couldn't understand what he was yelling about, so I would stare at him in terror, then make a new mistake. It was all a terribly repetitive process. By day four, I privately cried a couple of tears as I was filling up salt and pepper shakers in the basement, vowing never to visit the pyramids.

During this first week, I also began to get a sense of the people I would be serving. I realized working in the hotel was going to be far different than serving onion rings at Applebee's. For example, at the hotel I would walk around with a tray filled with gourmet, delicious hors d'oeuvres that cost five dollars a pop. Hors d'oeuvres that are basically a pile of fat and deliciousness in a compact package that I cannot stuff into my mouth behind curtains fast enough. The melted Brie cheese and raspberry on a sourdough cracker and the deep fried goat cheese stuffed artichoke hearts are my favorites. But when I offered these decadent treats to guests who are not interested, instead of a nice 'no thank you,' as one would expect, they turn their heads and pretend I am invisible.

One time while offering a man a very tasty 'frank en croute,' which is just an embarrassing, absurdly fancy way of saying 'pig in a blanket'; he remained silent, turned his head away with his nose high in the air, and shoved something in my pocket. Perhaps he was giving me a tip? Foolishly optimistic, I hurried to the back to see what present I was just awarded and realized he had shoved a chuck of chewed, spit up food wrapped in a napkin into my pocket. Are you freaking kidding me? My pocket is not your trash can, and excuse me while I go burn my tuxedo jacket and then bathe in sanitizer to get rid of your germs.

Fortunately, this guy was the only one who slipped me his cud, but the number of people who have ignored me after I offered them food were countless, and it never got less annoying or offensive. After the first couple times of experiencing the classic snobbery brush off, I began to pretend I just thought they didn't hear my polite offering. So, I would repeat it, louder and louder until I was almost shouting and the guest had no other choice but to acknowledge my question and look at my not-so-genuine smile. "Ma'am, would you care for a California roll? Ma'am, would you care for a California roll? MA'AM. CALIFORNIA ROLL?" Eventually I get a down-turned mouth, a pathetically murmured "no thank you." Hey, at least it was a response, a physical acknowledgement that I was indeed alive and not just an invisible ghost wrapped in a tuxedo that had been eternally damned to an afterlife of waitress servitude. Oh, the horror.

The prime example of Palm Beach craziness came one sunny day the first week of work, poolside. I was working a very popular charity event where everyone was required to dress in all white. The entire pool deck was a sea of bleached linen dresses, silicon body parts, and expensive loafers with no socks. As I walked toward the kitchen to pick up some food, a hotel guest stopped me and asked, "Is that a cult meeting?" I couldn't blame her for thinking so. The mass of white outfits did imply that the signature cocktail of the evening would be a funky Kool-Aid martini.

I continued into the kitchen to pick up what I would be passing out for the evening: delicious scallops wrapped in bacon, a little pool of grease forming around each one on the plate. So, so good, yet so, so bad. I emerged back into the mass of tan bodies and white outfits, and offered the greased sea muscle to a lady wearing a Tiffany's starfish necklace. She popped one into her mouth and exclaimed in her thick New York accent, "Oh, my, gawsh. This is the best thing I have ever eaten. Can I have another?" A little bit of bacon was stuck on her bottom lip.

"Of course, ma'am!" I replied, eager to get rid of them anyway and happy to encounter a nice human being.

Her short, dark purple manicured nails reached in to grab another scallop. But just then, a man with a canary yellow sweater wrapped around his narrow shoulders swooped in from the east, his eyes fiercely fixed on my plate of deliciousness. He went straight for the kill, reminding me of a cheetah I saw hunting an ostrich on Animal Planet the night before. The man wanted a scallop, and he wanted one that instant. His hand quickly slid over the plate, picked up a scallop and carried it towards his dry, crusty old man lips. But he abruptly stopped when he noticed the other woman reaching in for her round two scallop at precisely the same time. The sweater man gasped, and turned his nose a little higher than it already was. It was now so far up I could see his professionally trimmed nose hairs.

He looked at the woman and barked, "Excuse me!" his nasally, almost British sounding voice carrying far over the pool deck. "Before you put your grubby hands all over those scallops again, do you think I could have one? Humph!" And with that, he slammed down his scallop on my tray, almost knocking it to the ground. He turned sharply and walked away in his clean, perfect loafers with no socks. His canary yellow cable knit sweater waved behind him like the cape of an evil villain.

Oh. My. Goodness.

The woman and I watched him huff and puff back into the crowd. We blinked a few times, our mouths slightly open and heads crooked a little to the left. This was the moment when I realized people like that actually do exist, and were not just mythical television creatures created by producers of reality shows containing the word "housewives" in the title. I realized I was a far cry from the Midwest. This was now my job, my life: this was Palm Beach.

After apologizing to the nice lady on behalf of the canary yellow sweater monster, she murmured, "I bet he beats his girlfriend at night." With that, she popped another scallop through her perfectly painted red lips and walked away.

Gloria Estefan Smells Like Happy Babies and Christmas

One perk of my job, I quickly realized after getting hired, is that sometimes people or companies use their mass amounts of cash and hire famous singers to put on full-blown concerts for their events. Just like when I hired Beyoncé to sing at my wedding. Wait, that never happened. My wedding entertainment was a DJ who had a beer belly, and disappeared just as I wanted to throw my bouquet. I still have no idea where he went. Anyway, that evening's event was a fundraiser for the Everglades National Park. The decorations were beautiful, with massive wildflower and moss centerpieces towering on the 100 tables that filled the ballroom.

A large stage was set up in the front of the room, so I knew something fierce was about to go down. I looked at my paper that explained the evening's events, and I saw two words synonymous for 'good time' - Gloria Estefan. Cue the conga music that makes me shake my tuxedo-covered tail feather. So exciting.

We finished setting the tables, folding napkins, and polishing all the glasses just in time for the guests to start pouring in. I could hear the word Gloria being murmured at every table, her pending performance obviously a hot topic of the evening. I made my way to the kitchen to pick up some wine for my tables, and BAM. There she was, behind the stage – Gloria herself in all brilliance. Her hair extra curly, extra bouncy. Her height, extra short. I walked by her and SMACK. I am hit in the face with her scent. Yes, her scent. The chick smelled like an angel. From her wafted the loveliest blend of fragrant flowers mixed with the smell of my mom's Christmas cookies, fresh baby and a hint of love. She smelled so good it was weird. We made eye contact, and she smiled and said, "Hola!"

Oh my gosh – she spoke to me. This was the first celebrity I had ever seen and she was talking to me. This was one of those moments I would always daydream about in math class or some other God-forsaken place of boredom. In those dreams, I always imagined myself playing it cool, not getting overly excited because hey, they are just people like the rest of us, right?

I took a moment to mentally collect myself, and opened my mouth to respond to the beautiful, wonderful, talented Gloria Estefan.

"Why hello there, Mrs. Estefan, it is so nice to meet you. I am very much looking forward to your performance tonight. I have always been a fan of your music! I must run, but have a great show!"

FALSE. That is not what I said at all. If I could turn back the clock and have a celebrity encounter re-do, perhaps those would have been the words I spoke. But instead, me, an extremely awkward human with crooked teeth and a weak chin, did this:

I murmured, I stammered, and then finally I managed to say, "Hi, Gloria… ah… hey… you smell good!"

Her perfectly waxed brows scrunched together as she looked at me like the dork I was, and I ducked out to get those bottles of wine.

Really? I tell Gloria Freaking Estefan she smells good? Ridiculous. My lack of confidence probably stemmed from the fact that my tuxedo pants were so short you can see my faded black tube socks underneath. Or the fact that my shoes were nonstick grandma loafers I recently purchased at K-mart. (Grandma loafers make the best waitress shoes, trust me. If they can keep Granny grounded as she shuffles around, they can keep me from slipping in restaurant kitchen floor sludge.) Anyway, good smelling Gloria went on to conga-shake-shimmy the night away, and when I poured wine it often splashed onto the tablecloth, a result of me discreetly shaking my booty to her funky beats. I tried to forget my embarrassing encounter and lose myself in her Latin musical genius. It was an amazing performance, and I began to think I actually might enjoy this job… but probably not.

Don't Pop my Implant

The hotel was hosting a convention for local plastic surgeons. It was a low budget event and not highly decorative, with the extent of décor being sandalwood colored tablecloths covering the tables and a single candle burning in their centers. To me, this translated to boring and ugly. Once you whipped out those tan tablecloths, there was no turning back. Boring.[1] But then the guests arrived, and things got a little more, shall we say... interesting. The room became decorated by a sea of perfect silicon body parts dressed in skimpy couture outfits that showed off more skin than Lady Gaga in her worst/best moment. Welcome to the convention of people who look fake. It was cosmetic surgery heaven (or maybe hell? Either way, it was terrifying). Every woman had been tweaked, pulled, prodded and plumped. Granted, some looked good, but most were sliced and diced to the point where they looked like they arrived at the party in a space ship, chanting "take me to your surgeon" and armed with syringes of silicon.

I was standing at attention with my cocktail tray in hand, fully prepared to be the best waitress the world had ever seen, when a guest came up to me and said something, but I couldn't really understand her. It looked like she was practicing to become a ventriloquist, her face frozen and her massive plump

---

[1] What is with the word 'sandalwood' anyway? It reminds me of a chalky shoe worn in ancient Egyptian times that smells like a horse's butt, which pretty much describes how exciting the color is as well. Death to beige, forever! Death to beige!

lips barley moving as she attempted to speak. Oh Botox, you are so weird. I leaned in close to try and decipher her murmurs. I was pretty sure I heard the word 'martini', so I headed straight to the bar to get her one. Obviously this woman could use a drink, her face was so stiff it looked like she just swapped spit with Jack Frost. The only time my face has ever been that frozen is when I stayed out ice fishing too long with my dad when it was 20 degrees below zero.[2]

Forty-five minutes of the cocktail-serving drudgery went by, and people began taking their seats at the banquet tables. The MC for the night went on stage to begin the award ceremony. His hair was perfectly coifed like a Ken doll, and his bright white (probably fake) teeth were almost too blinding to look at. His skin was smooth, clean-shaven, and topped with the perfect shade of spray tan. His beauty was terrifying, downright terrifying.

He began reading through the awards that were going to be given away, flashing his pearly whites after every category. Top prizes would go to those who looked the most different from their high school yearbook photo and those whose nose most closely resembled Michael Jackson's.[3] Okay, that is a lie, they were boring medical awards nobody actually cared about. If I described them to you, you would probably fall asleep like a narcoleptic, they were that un-interesting.

The Ken Doll read the first award and its recipient. "And the winner is…" he said in his best, cheesy MC voice, "Sherry Peachtree!"

Is that a real name?

A squeal erupted from the audience, and a lady, whom one could only assume to be Ms. Peachtree, jumped up and

---

[2] I caught a bass, and we fried it for dinner, and my face eventually thawed, in case you were concerned, which I am sure you were not, you selfish, selfish reader you.

[3] RIP of King of Pop. I will forever remember those sleepovers dancing like total dorks with my friends to Billy Jean. And by the way, where did you get that red jacket you wore in Thriller? Me wants one.

down like a high school cheerleader on cocaine and red bull. She was wearing an extremely tight, fully sequined hot-pink strapless dress. Her hair was so big and blonde it looked like she arrived straight from Texas. She continued to squeal and giggle as she made her way to the stage to receive her award, her feet taking tiny, careful steps in her five-inch heels. The MC had a purple ribbon in his hands, and when the Peachtree arrived you could almost see the sheer excitement in his eyes as he reached in to pin it onto her massive chest. There was not much fabric to attach it to, so there were three whole seconds of his hands floating around, looking for a place a pin could even stick.

But just as Ken Doll started to attach the award to her dress, the woman's bleached blond head bobbled in toward the mike, and she proclaimed in front of 400 people, "Don't pop my implant!" and she let out an insufferable giggle that sounded like Fran Drescher with a bad case of laryngitis.[4]

When I heard those words amplified over the entire ballroom, I almost dropped an entire tray of salad into the teased coif of a guest. Did she actually just yell that out in front of hundreds of people and then laugh about it like she was the next Dane Cook? She did, and she need felt no embarrassment, as I felt it all for her. I think the crowd was smiling, but it was hard to tell because the almighty Botox froze most of their faces in time. A light laughter was heard flitting around the room, but it wasn't enough to salve the aftermath of such a weird comment. In fact, you would probably need a chainsaw to cut through the uncomfortable silence blanketing the ballroom. But alas, Sherry Peachtree seemed not to notice or care; her eyes glinted as bright as her rhinestone encrusted gown as she returned to her seat donning her new award.

There are three life-changing morals of this story-
1.Fake chests must be handled with care. Contents may explode when punctured. 2.Never, ever attend a plastic surgery convention. 3.If your name is Sherry Peachtree, or anything of

---

[4] I know every word to the theme song of *The Nanny*, and if you pay me five dollars I will sing it to you. Ten dollars and I will record it on a CD.

similar perkiness, you have a free pass to yell whatever you want into a microphone. Enjoy.

Epic Nuptials

Oh, weddings. A time for love, a time for happiness, and a time for spending large amounts of money on a day that will pass quicker than a popcorn fart. Most weddings at the hotel are completely over the top on the scale of matrimonial extravagance. I mean, let's get real. If you can even afford to put a down payment to reserve the ballroom, you can probably afford everything else your little bridal heart desires. A clan of magical elves wearing purple afro wigs to serve your wedding cake? Sure! It fits in the budget.

One thing that always amazes me about weddings at the hotel is how much food is served. People on the island spend thousands upon thousands of dollars on liposuction, plastic surgery, personal trainers, and anything else that is guaranteed to give you the body of an underfed Greek goddess. But when a wedding is held, they bring in enough food to send an entire cast of The Biggest Loser into an obesity relapse. Usually a heavy hors d'oeuvre reception kicks off the night. An artistically sculpted pile of cheese, fruit and crackers will sit in the middle of the room, big enough to put even the French to shame. A massive raw bar will be laid out, with so many dead oysters and shrimps the ecosystem of the Atlantic could be permanently affected. Then we, the tuxedo serving bandits, will pass out a million and one hot hors d'oeuvres. Mini grilled cheese sandwiches with shots of hot tomato soup, fried artichoke hearts stuffed with goat cheese, tiny little Cuban sandwiches - it is endless. And delicious. Now remember, that is just the cocktail hour. Next up is the five course dinner. A beet and goat cheese salad drizzled with balsamic reduction to start. Next, a warm crab cake on a bed of arugula that is so greasy and fluffy and perfect I almost drool on the guests as I serve it. Sometimes a sorbet course is served next. Can we talk about that for a minute? Who thought it was a good idea to serve the tiniest scoop of ice cream in between courses? I don't care how fancy you are – a mini frozen treat mid-dinner is just weird.

After that stupid course, we bring out the big guns with the main entrée, which usually consists of a filet mignon, extremely fattening mashed potatoes, an adorable mini skillet of bubbling hot mac and cheese, and perhaps one stem of asparagus for good measure. And then to complete the obesity fest, we present dessert – my favorite being a gigantic ice cream sundae served in an oversized martini class, with little waffle cone cups of toppings to dump on top of it. Bliss, pure sugary bliss. And don't forget about the wedding cake, which, for the record, doesn't count as a course.

But wait! It does not end there. Often there is post-dinner food that needs to be passed. After the guests have about an hour to semi-digest their massive meal and have danced off about one tenth of the calories consumed, we bring out delectable treats like freshly baked chocolate chip cookies served with a shot glass of icy cold milk, chocolate dipped key lime pie on a stick, or chocolate covered cheesecake bites. However, the post-dinner food is not always dessert. Brides sometimes order a round of our most greasy, delicious food in a feeble attempt to sober up their wedding guests before they hit the roads. Things can and have gotten ugly at this point. The overfed guests have literally gotten angry with me for offering them food, otherwise known as just doing my job. Who knew the sight of a mini grilled cheese sandwich could evoke such rage?

Here is an example of what the dialogue between my guests and me may look like on a night of such edible excess:

Cocktail hour, early into the evening:
Me: "Hors d'oeuvres, ma'am?"

Guest: "Oh, I shouldn't, but what the heck, it's a wedding!" And she shoves five deviled eggs past her perfectly painted lips.

First Course:
Guest: "Oh, is that goat cheese?"
Me: "Yes ma'am! With candied walnuts, beets and pears on a bed of spinach with raspberry vinaigrette."
Guest: "Oh, it looks delicious!" And she licks her plate clean like a Neanderthal.

Second Course:
Guest: "Is this lobster bisque?"
Me: "Yes ma'am, it is, complete with massive amounts of cream and butter."
Guest: "Is it fattening?"
Me: "No. And by no, I mean yes, very." And she drinks it all through a straw. One button on her gown flies off.

Third Course:
Guest: "Why do they serve these weird mini sorbets in the middle of dinner?"
Me: "I have no idea."

Fourth Course:
Guest: "What is this filet mignon stuffed with?"
Me: "Crab meat, cheese, calories and lard."
Guest: Already shoving the steak down her throat, no time to respond.

Fifth Course:
Me: "Here is your massive ice cream sundae, with your choice of five candy toppings! Would you like caramel sauce or chocolate sauce with that?"
Guest: "I don't think I could eat another bite!" And she glares at me for offering her the most delicious dessert in the world. But then starts eating it anyway.

Sixth Course:
Me: "Wedding cake, ma'am?"
Guest: "What nerve you have even offering! We are all full, thank you, now move along!" She huffs and puffs at the thought of eating another morsel, and four more buttons fly off.

Post dinner hors d'oeuvres:
Me: Would you care for... SMACK. The guest slaps me across the face, and her husband rolls her fat body back to the hotel room where she passes out in a sugar coma.

Because some bride got food ordering happy, I became the evil one. I became the one that made them have to add on an extra two hours with Claude the Swedish trainer just to burn off all the excess calories they consumed. Listen, you cranky, bloated guest with garlic breath – don't blame me! Blame the woman in the white dress on the dance floor getting down to Katy Perry songs with her college roommates.

But it is not always the food that is over the top at weddings. Often, the entertainment can be outlandish as well. Once, a groom had secretly arranged a firework show to go off right after he and his new bride had shared their vows. It was a sweet gesture, I suppose. However, a lot goes into planning your own personal fireworks display. First, he needed to rent a barge to drive out into the ocean to launch them from, which in itself seemed like a daunting task. Then there were all these permits he had to get to be able to legally launch explosives into the sky, in addition to buying the fireworks themselves. Craig shared with us that the entire bill for the fireworks show was over $200,000 dollars. Oh. My. Goodness. However, there is one thing money cannot buy: a clear weather forecast.

The morning of the wedding it was already apparent the climate was going to be less than ideal for outdoor nuptials. The sky was a wall of grey, no hopeful breaks of blue in sight. As the day progressed, the sky got darker and darker, until finally, at around 3:00 in the afternoon, a raindrop hit me in the forehead as I was walking into the hotel. Followed by several more, and a loud clap of thunder. It was now clear the outdoor wedding reception and surprise firework display was not going to happen. Did the man get his money back? Nope. Turned out, rented barges and explosives are non-refundable. No big deal, it's only $200,000 right? Chump change. Pause – I just had a mini panic attack thinking about wasting $200,000 on NOTHING. Okay, I have recovered. Moving on.

You would think at this point, the man would give up on his 'wedding surprises,' after literally just throwing hundreds of thousands of dollars into the ocean. But no, he was not finished. He was determined to shock his bride and give her a wedding she could never forget. The groom pulled a few strings and ended up hiring aerial dancers to make grand entrances from the ceiling during the reception. However, these were not your everyday ribbon acrobats, they were ex-Cirque du Soleil performers – only the best for his little bride to be.

So the ceremony, now moved indoors, came and went. Guests began pouring into the reception, which was now taking place in the only ballroom we had available for the night, which is by far the ugly stepchild of our ballroom selection. The bride seemed extra social and in good spirits despite her wedding being moved from a gorgeous oceanfront courtyard to a room with retractable walls. She was making her way around the crowd, greeting everyone warmly and looking happy. Then, about twenty minutes into the meet and greet, loud, deep bass music started playing and the lights dimmed. Spotlights shone in the corners of the room. Curtains that had been set up were pulled back, revealing four acrobats winding and twirling their way through the air on long, white stretches of fabric.

I was watching the bride at this point, as that was her big 'wedding surprise' moment. Would she gasp, cover her mouth, then run to her husband and embrace him in gratitude for his thoughtfulness? Would she cry, laugh, or watch in wonderment at the amazing acrobatics? No. She did none of these things. She briefly glanced at the spandex-clad performers suspended high in the air over her wedding reception, gave them a confused, 'what the heck is that' type of a look, similar to a look one would give when coming across a unidentifiable crispy object in your French fries that obviously is not made out of potato.

Then she continued making her greeting rounds, and didn't look at the performers again.

I saw the groom standing in the corner, obviously confused as to why his bride was more interested in her Aunt Peggy than his pricey surprise. He walked over to the bar and ordered a whisky. After a failed firework attempt and a failed airborne acrobatic performer attempt, what else is there to do but drink a whisky? Cheers to you, new husband, and may you have many more years of trying to meet your new bride's expectations.

Your Poodle Freaks the Crap Out of Me

On my days off, one of my favorite things to do is go to the West Palm Beach public library. Screw the beach - I want literature! It is only about fifteen blocks from my house, so some days I bike, walk, or run there. One day, I was feeling particularly flabby, so I decided to speed up my slow meander into a brisk jog. The only problem was, I had a purse full of books to be returned. It was a bag that slung over one shoulder, across the body and sat next to my hip. I decided it shouldn't be too difficult to jog with, so my attempt at exercise began.

A few blocks later, a car slowed down and pulled up next to me. A middle-aged man with thinning dark hair rolled down his window. I continued jogging and simultaneously reached into my bag and fumbled around to find my pepper spray. That was the moment I have prepared myself for - the moment of my abduction. I would not become the subject of the next episode of *48 Hours Mystery*. You'd better watch out, sketchy car driver, I will not hesitate to use my peppery weapon.

The man spoke to me.

"Miss, are you in an emergency?"

Oh, I see. He sees my purse, an unusual jogging accessory, and thought I was running for my life, perhaps from some unseen predator, or perhaps because I have a serious intestinal problem that needed immediate attention.

"Ah, nope… just jogging," I told him, as my freckled face turned red. He drove away, and I slowed to a walk. Did my feeble crack at exercise really look that pathetic and helpless? I was just trying to burn some calories. Sigh.

It was on another one of those walks to the library when I first witnessed something that made me want to punch myself in the left eye. I was walking along peacefully, thinking about how I wanted to check out a vegetarian cookbook. For some reason, I thoroughly enjoy reading vegetarian cookbooks, although I eat meat fairly regularly. I guess I just like to toy with the idea of eliminating the consumption of flesh from my diet, but never have enough energy to do so. I bought soy-based pepperoni once. Five dollars and one weird tasting pizza later, I regretted my decision and made myself a turkey sandwich, preservatives and all.

Anyway, I was walking to the library and had stopped at an intersection while waiting for the light to change. A woman pushing a stroller was also standing there. She was wearing a massive wide-brimmed hat and pink Chanel sunglasses – probably the real kind, not some cheap, sidewalk vendor knockoff. I peeked into her stroller expecting to see a chubby cute baby, probably dressed in adorable baby-sized designer clothes. But when I laid my eyes on the creature encased in said stroller, I gasped in horror. That was either the single most hairy baby known to man, or the woman was pushing around a poodle in the stroller. She spotted me gazing at her four-legged friend, and I was forced to make conversation. "Cute… dog?" She looked at me, didn't smile, didn't say thank you – just stared me down like I was an idiot.

Thank goodness at that moment the light changed and we were able to cross the street and hurry away from each other. What is going on? Why on earth would it ever be a good idea to push a dog around in a stroller? Breaking news everybody – a dog's entire day revolves around going for a walk. If you don't walk your dog, it becomes clinically depressed and probably a little suicidal. DOGS LOVE WALKS. So unless the creature was a paraplegic, there was no excuse to push him around in a stroller. None.

But the stroller wasn't the only thing that bothered me about that situation. Not only was she acting like a crazy woman for treating a dog like an infant child, but also the dog was a

POODLE. Listen, I love dogs, I adore them. My parents own a golden retriever who has been trained to throw my Dad's empty beer bottles into the recycling. But poodles... yikes. Let's get real – poodles are not dogs, just a bad haircut with legs. The little ones alone are terrifying, and the standard sizes reach a whole new level of ridiculous. Why are they so large and why do they have shaved legs with little tufts of hair around their ankles? There is no excuse for ankle tufts, ever. There is nothing right about this.

Once, while at the dog park with a friend and her chocolate lab, a massive black poodle, afro puffs and all, was prancing about like a hot mess. That dog did not move like other dogs. While the lab, bulldogs and mutts were zipping across the park, chasing balls or each other, the black giant poodle looked more like he was performing a scene from Swan Lake. He did not run; rather he leapt across the open field, his long legs jetting into the air with the grace of an oddly feminine male French dancer, likely named Pierre. It was just not right.

I don't understand why the wealthy are generally known for purchasing these odd companions. The rest of their world is full of beautiful things, but when it comes to dogs they seem to pick out the weirdest and most terrifying one on the market. I blogged about my distaste for poodles once and a Palm Beacher, who identified himself only as 'Mister Johnny,' left a comment about the poodle catastrophe in his own neighborhood. I could not have received a better comment from anybody, about anything, ever. Here is what he said:

"A dozen years ago, on the North End, there was a woman with two huge standard sized 'accessory' poodles. One was named Flaubert and the other one also had a French artist's name. Anyway, they were not trained at all. They were jumpers. They ran wild over the North End. One even took to defecating in my pool! Yuck! Like drunks from a late night at the bar Cucina, I often saw the police taking these poodles back to this woman's house after a run through the neighborhood."

Flaubert, the pool-pooping poodle. I about coughed up a lung laughing when I read that. And although Flaubert had a disconcerting bowel problem, you do have to give him props for having such a hilarious name.

I ran into another poodle, perhaps it was Flaubert, while shopping at the island's grocery store. I hate going into that grocery store. Every woman in there is dressed like a model, their stilettos clicking across the hard floors and their oversized sunglasses remaining on their face for the entire duration of their shopping experience. I usually only go there if I am on my way home from the beach and am in desperate need of a grocery item. My face typically makeup-less, and my hair a frizzy mess. I usually am seventy-eight percent covered in sand, and have wet spots on the boob area of my tank-top from my still drying bathing suit underneath. But, nevertheless, I needed my half-gallon of organic milk to make my latte the next morning, so I sucked it up and grocery shopped with my ugliness in full view.

That time, I was buying hot dogs for an upcoming camping trip to St. Augustine, which in my opinion is the best city in Florida. (Sorry, West Palm.) I was rounding the corner to head down aisle five when I came face to face with a three-foot tall, massive white poodle. His afro puff hair was larger than Tina Turner's on her best day. I was so taken aback by this creature being in the grocery store that I almost dropped my mystery meat sticks wrapped in synthetic cellulose casings. The dog and I locked eyes for about four seconds, when it raised its leg and peed on a display of canned tomatoes, staring at me the entire time as if to say "I wish I was peeing on you instead." The owner just glanced at the puddle of urine and kept on shopping, too interested in filling her entire shopping cart full of overpriced wine than to bother with her dogs bodily functions.

While camping that weekend, I thought I was far enough away from Palm Beach to avoid running into any other fancy prancing, pool pooping, tomato can peeing beasts, but I was wrong. Even in the north part of Florida, where people live a "simpler life" and enjoy shooting pythons on the weekends, these premed canines roam free. Kyle and I were setting up our tent at the Hicksville Campground[5] when an employee came rolling up to our site on a golf cart to tell us about karaoke in the rec hall that evening. (All the best campgrounds have nightly rec-hall karaoke, obviously.) The woman was missing one of her front teeth, and was wearing an oversized neon greet T-shirt that had a lake scene printed on its front. It had an extra wide neck hole, so the shirt slung low off one of her chubby shoulders, revealing much more of her mole-covered skin than I cared to see. Sitting there next to her were two miniature poodles, dark gray in color. They had matching polka dot bows pinned to each of their stinky ears, and their doggie nails were grown all the way out and painted an obnoxious, tacky shade of red. That was too much for me, just too much. When I see human beings with long red fingernails I get freaked out, let alone POODLES with such an ungodly manicure choice. Turns out no matter where you go, people will always be, well, people. And that means they will be weird… and own poodles.

---

[5] Not the actual name, but the owners should consider changing it to be so, as it most accurately describes their facilities. When we drove in, we passed an old guy in a rocking chair. He met eyes with us, and then gave us the middle finger for no reason. Why we didn't take that as a sign to find another place to stay, I don't know.

Business Socks = Adultery

Oh drunks, you are so silly. I was working the after party to some big corporate event that rounded up hundreds of businessmen and brought them far away from their families and normal responsibilities of life, pumped them with free alcohol, and left them to run free like in the days of their youth. They were the kind of businessmen that wore black socks with stiff leather loafers. At the end of the day, those black socks would be saturated with sweat from sitting through hours of meetings. Once the leather shoes were removed, a stench so foul it should be classified as hazardous would fill the entire room. You know what I am talking about. I hate black stinky businessman socks. I hate them.

It was after dinner and well into the evening. Everyone left lingering in the room was quite boozy. There was a man dressed in an expensive looking business suit, repulsive black socks and gold wedding ring leaning up against the bar. He was obnoxiously flirting with a woman who was clearly not his wife. Next to the woman was her mother, a soft woman in her sixties wearing feisty red lipstick. Of course, the drunken businessman was flirting with her as well. He was leaning up on the bar, and apparently has mastered the art of talking normally while wasted, so the extent of his inebriation was not apparent, and the bartender kept the wine flowing.

But then, as best said in the old-school lyrical genius of Semisonic… closing time. The bartender began packing up for the evening, and us servers started loudly clearing cups and plates out of the room, a very passive aggressive way of saying, "please leave…now." The man slowly pushed himself up from the bar, and began to walk towards the door … kind of. He was so inebriated he was practically defying gravity, swirling around like a renegade pair of underwear caught in a tornado. He made seven woozy laps around the room before taking a break and leaning against the wall.

Seeing his pathetic intoxication, the mother-daughter pair he was collectively lusting for decided to be nice and allow him to lean on them as they tried to steer him out of the ballroom. As they approached the doors to exit, all of the servers stopped what we were doing, our heads perking up like markets spotting a lion in the distance. We all hurried out into the hallway after them, because we knew what was about to happen. We could smell a hot mess looming, and since there was little we could do to prevent the catastrophe at this point, we at least wanted a front row seat to the action. You see, right outside of the room was a lovely set of stairs, and the big drunk baboon with the women hooked on his arms was heading right for them. Cue: Beethoven's Fifth.

We tried to call out to them, tried to help, try to tell them not to descend, but it was too late. One step, two steps, aaaandddddddddddddd…… KER PLUNK.[6] The man dove head first, taking the women down with him and smashing his drunken noggin right into the cement wall.

So there they sat - mother, daughter and married drunk man flattened in the middle of one of the classiest hotels in America, their body parts all tangled together. But fear not, children, as this embarrassing situation does not end with this stumble tumble down the stairs. This man had a goal - a goal he was not going to give up on easily. This man wanted sex.

He and the women, clearly feeling a little numb from their previous booze session and not yet fully realizing the extent of their injuries, managed to stand themselves upright and

---

[6] If you didn't know, "ker plunk" is the sound a drunk man and two women make when they fall down stairs. It is also an amazingly awesome game that made my early 90's childhood years all the more awesome.

headed for the elevator. The ladies were still helping him walk, a very noble deed if I must say, considering he just caused them all to face plant into the ugly hotel carpet. The trio finally reached the elevator, and the ladies propped the man up to stand on his own.

The elevator dinged, the gold doors slid open and the drunk man stepped in between them, preventing them from closing. He then reached for the middle-aged woman's hand, and attempted to pull her into the elevator with him. She was not having it. She put her heels in the ground like a stubborn mule, obviously not in any way wanting to continue her evening with this befuddled adulterer. I watched in agony for a full sixty seconds as the man, clearly not getting the hint, kept attempting to pull the woman into the elevator with him. When he finally gave up on the tug of war game, the ladies started to walk away. But he was not yet done with his desperate attempts, as he then reached out and grabbed the elderly mother's arm, and again, proceeded to attempt to yank her into the elevator with him and up to his room. Awesome married businessman, really awesome. Well, if he couldn't snag the daughter, might as well go after the graying woman who gave birth to her. What's next, calling Great Grandma Ethel to see if she wants to party?

The mother, obviously fed up, jerked her arm away with such force that it threw the drunken man off balance, and he tumbled back into the elevator. The gold doors shut, and the women were finally free. They quickly turn and hurried down the hall, glancing back over their shoulders ever so often, perhaps double checking that the man didn't burst out of the elevator on a horse and lasso them.

It was a true moment of greatness for the businessman, one he and his family could be proud of. I am sure he received a promotion straight after this class act evening. Either that or a severance package.

Hot Dang This Christmas Party is Amazing

When I think of employee holiday parties, I used to envision a group of half bored, half exhausted co-workers crowding around a bowl of non-alcoholic punch, munching on semi-stale Christmas cookies that Sheri the receptionist baked, a few crumbs spilling onto their best button-up shirts. At least, that was how I pictured holiday parties until I began working at the hotel. Now when I think of them, what comes to mind is – the best night ever.

It was early November and I was polishing silverware with several other tuxedo-wearing bandits. I overheard some of them talking about a holiday party held at the hotel, and my interest was piqued.

"Does the hotel throw an employee Christmas party?" I asked, as I grabbed five more salad knives and inspected them for remnants of dried dishwasher residue.

"Ah, yeah," said Amos, a sixty-five year old Jamaican man that could single handedly polish silverware faster than any other human on the planet and had no sense of humor whatsoever.

"It is the best party you will ever go to in your life," he explained. "They give us the biggest ballroom, full band, five course meal, dancing, everything! Even…" he paused here to inspect a fork he was rubbing clean, "an open bar."

What? This is too good to be true. I put down my knives and went to hunt down Craig to get the scoop. I found him in the hallway alphabetically arranging 200 name cards for the night's event.

"Craig, do we get an employee holiday party?" I asked him as he bent over the table, trying to perfectly line up the row of last names starting with C.

"Yes, of course, now finish these name cards," he barked, as he handed me the remaining pile and hurried down the hallway. Craig often reminded me of a lemur hopped up on Red Bull.

Come December, the days leading up to the holiday party seemed to approach at the pace of a three-legged tortoise. I had not had this much anticipation for Christmas since I was nine years old, though for very different reasons. Back then I was waiting for an American Girl doll; now I was just excited to put on a dress and eat free cheese. My female co-workers and I put great thought into what we would wear to this grand event. I settled on a borrowed powder pink lace dress, lots of dramatic pearl necklaces and gold sparkly pumps. I could have worn a potato sack with a rip in it and still looked better than I do when I was wearing that darned tuxedo, so I felt pretty confident walking into the hotel that evening.

Kyle and I headed to the back foyer of the hotel where our hors d'oeuvre reception was to be held before we would be let in the ballroom for dinner. Everything was set up exactly how it would be if we were the most important guests the hotel had ever had. Every table was topped with glowing votive candles and covered in floor-length red damask tablecloths. Three full bars were set up, and a fruit and cheese display sat in the middle of the room. Since there are nearly 2,000 employees at the hotel, the party was split up into two nights. While that night I would be wining and dining as if I were a Kennedy, the following day I would be back to the reality of tuxedo-clad servant-hood, passing food and drinks to my co-workers and sweating under the weight of my heavy, polyester fashion faux-pas.

But this was far from my mind at this point, for at this one moment I was a guest at the hotel, something I never thought would be possible. I was the one being waited on. I was the one being served delicious delectables like baked Brie cheese and raspberry on sourdough bread, or greasy fried coconut chicken fingers. The best part was, I could eat them out in the open and not have to fear retribution. There would be no hiding in the back kitchen cooler at that party. No, that night I was going to eat a like real human being, at a table, with a fork and knife and even a napkin. I was elated.

As the reception continued, the room filled quickly. Every co-worker was allowed to bring a guest, so there were plenty of faces I did not recognize, but several that I did. I noticed there were lots of people from school there, and I wondered whom they were attending with. I ran into a group of them near one of the bars, and saw one of my good friends, Dave. Dave has a heart of gold, but a head of insanity. He is known for doing outrageously crazy things, like the time he decided to jump off the bridge over the Intercostal Waterway that connects the mainland to Palm Beach. This is no quick jump into a pool, but an extremely long drop into unknown waters below, which very well may contain sharks, gators, or dead bodies. Dave jumped in and survived, so from the dark waters below he yelled to his partner in crime, Kara, to take the plunge as well. Dave and Kara are like two extremely destructive peas in a pod. They were always together, always causing trouble, and always making us laugh.

Kara, on the edge of the bridge, was hesitant, but could not let Dave show her up, so she jumped. As she did, one of her feet slipped and her balance was thrown off. Instead of plugging her nose and making a perfect pencil dive into the water, Kara's body went horizontal, meaning she was about to experience the biggest belly flop known to man. She screamed all the way down, her windblown flesh making a loud slapping sound when it hit the water. When she resurfaced, she let out a howl of pain as Dave almost sank from laughing so hard. The pair swam to the edge of the water and began climbing the concrete wall to get out, only to discover it was covered in barnacles. After painfully trying to scale the wall, they finally hit dry land, and the bottoms of their feet were more cut up than a ham at a New York deli. But they laughed the whole way home, considered the night a success, and they tucked it away into their vault of crazy stories.

But that night at the party, Dave looked handsome and put together in a navy blue suit and a bright orange tie. He had a beer in one hand and a whiskey in the other. There were some crumbs on his face from his recent trip to the cheese platter, which I was about to tackle myself.

"Hey!" I said to him, with a punch to the arm in greeting. "Who are you here with?"

"Oh, a bunch of us heard about the party, and just parked down the road and walked in the back," he said, flashing me his toothy grin. Crashing the hotel holiday party - I liked this concept. I scanned the crowd and noticed about a five to one college student to actual employee ratio. I also recognized a maid who was surrounded by her four kids and husband, far exceeding the 'plus one' invitational limit. It seemed that sneaking into this thing was a little too easy, and the room was getting more crowded by the second. Well, just as long as I got my filet mignon dinner, I would be happy. I left Dave just as he was ordering a round of drinks.

After loading up a cocktail napkin with slices of Brie cheese, cheddar cubes, raspberries and crackers, Kyle and I headed inside to find a seat, as the reception was ending and the dinner was about to begin.

We managed to find a table near Dave and my good friend Coco. I was introduced to CoCo at school soon after I moved to Florida, and we both got our jobs at the same time. When I met her she had just given her heart to Jesus, her newfound faith saving her from an empty life of self-destructive choices. She has a kind heart, and could always make me laugh. She smokes way too many cigarettes, and drinks diet green tea out of big 24-ounce cans, and then uses them as ashtrays. Her hair is bleached blonde, and when she wears red lipstick she looks like Lady Gaga, but she hates if you tell her that. I absolutely love her. I love Lady Gaga. I love them both, and would love CoCo even more if she wore a meat dress.

We were lucky to find seats by them, as the room was filling at a speedy rate. The on-duty servers frantically circled the tables pouring champagne, merlot and chardonnay. Dave accepted the offer of all three, while the rest of us had to pass as we were not yet twenty-one and were strongly lectured beforehand that we would be fired if caught drinking – Lame.com.

The first course was served; a caramelized pear on a bed of arugula sprinkled with blue cheese, candied walnuts and drizzled with balsamic vinaigrette. I ate it slowly, savoring every single bite, simply because I could. The next course was filet mignon and panko-crusted white halibut in a cream sauce, with baby carrots and a skillet of macaroni and cheese, which is always my favorite. I swear to you, they pack more cheese in that tiny skillet than Kraft produces in one day. Plus, the baby-sized pan is so adorable that it adds to the deliciousness. I can just picture a garden gnome cooking up some mean pancakes on it in his tree stump home.

Finally it came time for dessert, and we were served a chocolate molten lava cake with fresh strawberries and vanilla bean ice cream. So freaking delicious. The chocolate gooey center of that perfectly round cake made me want to tap dance upon consumption, but I resisted.

After every delectable morsel was licked from our plates, we moved to another ballroom for a big old dance party. Nothing makes for a better party than an open bar, tons of party-crashing college kids and your strange co-workers. The hotel's best band was set up on stage, belting out the latest pop hits. The room was dim except for a massive disco ball over the dance floor and dozens of candles scattered throughout. There was a dessert buffet set up in the corner, and an espresso station with a real live barista to whip out our favorite coffee creations upon request. They spared no expense for us. This was the real deal. We were treated exactly as if we were the highest paying guests, and it felt amazing.

Dave, now fairly intoxicated (although I know he would be doing the same sober), was in the middle of the floor whipping out the most God-awful dance moves known to man. The sprinkler, the shopping cart— basically he was doing everything an immature seventh grade class clown that forgot to take his Ritalin would be doing at a school dance. The only difference was Dave happened to be the ripe age of twenty-seven, and in the middle of a classy party, but whatev. Let the good times roll.

Besides Dave and his performance, there was a pair of co-workers making out in the corner who probably should not have been, and even crotchety old Amos was getting his groove on full throttle. It was a glorious, chaotic sight.

Three hours of intense dancing and espresso sipping later, the music stopped, the lights turned on, and we all headed to our cars to make the reality trip back to our dingy, overpriced apartments on the mainland. As Kyle and I were walking out, we saw a group of our friends pointing up to the top of the hotel and laughing hysterically. We joined them and followed their gaze to see what was so funny. There, on top of one of the hotel's two towers, was Dave, holding the iconic flag with the hotel's logo on it in his hand. He had somehow managed to find his way up to this high peak, and now stood there like King Kong, holding the flag out in drunken victory. I was terrified for his safety, yet had to laugh at the same time. Only Dave would have had the desire to attempt such a feat, and have equal parts smarts, stupidity and bravery to execute it.

He made his way down the tower safely, and snuck the flag out of the hotel tucked in his jacket. It now hangs on his apartment wall, a memento of his brave climbing adventure, and of the best holiday party known to man. I could hardly wait for next December to arrive so I could throw on another fancy dress and dance away the mundaneness of the poor college student life.

But when we all returned from Christmas break and got back to work, we were harshly informed there would be no more holiday parties. We were all completely heartbroken. Craig explained it was because of the recession and the hotel had to cut some things out of the budget. Darn you, you stinky, festering recession! First you take our cash and hope in America, then you take our free wine and food? Will you show no mercy? But despite Craig's believable explanation as to why the party would be no more, I was sure the influx of un-invited college students and the hairless gorilla climbing the hotel's tower may have had something to do with the cancellation. Oh well, I guess next year we will just all have to buy ugly Christmas sweaters from Goodwill, crowd around a bowl of punch and nibble on semi-stale grocery store cookies. Life is hard.

Guido Wedding of the Century

This tale hails from before the days of America's *Jersey Shore* obsession. Before Snookie was blinding everyone with her orange skin and late night talk show hosts were taught how to pump their fist by a creature named "The Situation." This is a tale of another group of Guidos on the day of their holy matrimony.

I arrived at work early because I was assigned to be the bridal attendant for the evening. Being a bridal attendant is fun... sort of. You get to be in the room as the bride and her bridesmaids are getting ready, and do extremely important tasks such as filling up their bowl of pretzels and straightening out their bottles of Cokes so all the labels face the same way. You hold her bouquet for her as she walks down the hall, and help smooth the train of her gown as she poses for pictures. To be completely honest, the most fun part of it all is when they tip you at the end of the night.

I walked into the hotel's small beachside restaurant where the reception was going to take place. It was an intimate space next to the pool with a beautiful view of the Atlantic. Cocktail hour was usually outside on the patio, with a salty sea breeze providing relief from the hot Florida weather. Dinner took place right inside, the dozen or so tables skirted around the edges of the room to allow for the band and a dance floor in the center.

Tonight the room was decorated elegantly. The tables were covered with cream silk tablecloths, their trendy but classic embroidered damask pattern visible in the soft candlelight. Large circular mirrors lay underneath massive light pink and white flower arrangements that stood four feet tall, crystals dangling from the willow branches bursting out of their center. Candles were everywhere on the tables, lining the perimeter of the room and hanging in glass globes suspended over the dance floor, casting a warm romantic haze and contrasting shadows on the walls. The room looked like every girl's wedding dream, and I thought whoever designed the event must be classy, beautiful, and tasteful. This night was bound to be the perfect wedding. If only I knew the fate that lay ahead of me, if only I knew.

Just then, Craig burst through the kitchen doors. "Katie, the bridal suite is room 503. The couple is from New York." He pauses and swallows hard. "Good luck," he said with a look of fear in his eyes, and he scurried back into the kitchen. Craig was so odd. Surely the couple was just another pair of high society Manhattan hot shots; this should be like any other night. I was excited to go see if the bride looked like a Barbie doll, as most of the other ones did, so I headed upstairs.

I got in the elevator and pressed floor five. I always felt a little uncomfortable going up to the guest floors, as much of my work was usually confined to the depths of the basement or in stinky kitchens. I was not used to feeling such plush carpet beneath my feet, and I noticed the walls of the hallway were soft and padded like an insane asylum. Coincidence? I think not.

As I approached room 503, I heard yelling coming from behind the off-white wooden door. Confused, I double-checked the piece of paper where I had scribbled the room number down, as I have the memory of a goldfish and have been known to forget my own mother's birthday[7]. Yes, the room with all the screaming was indeed the bridal suite. I was slightly terrified, but curious all the same, so I knocked.

The door flew open, and there stood the bride. She was extremely fat, and I immediately noticed a purple cheetah tattoo on her left shoulder. Her hair was spun in tight ringlets all

---

[7] Sorry again about that Mom – whoops!

around her face, and her dress had more poof to it than Glenda the Good Witch's in The *Wizard of Oz.*

"Uh, hello there!" I stammered, momentarily distracted by her unusual appearance. "Ah ... congratulations! Can I get you anything?" I was afraid the answer was going to be cigarettes and a six-pack of Natty Ice.

"Yeah, a groom who isn't an idiot!" she snapped at me. With that she yelled a few expletives over her shoulder, and the "idiot" groom emerged from around the corner.

"Shut up, Lisa!" he barked. More curse words were exchanged.

The groom's hair was asphalt black and gelled into thick, chunky spikes that stood perfectly erect over his unshaven face. Multiple gold chains hung around his neck, all clearly visible because the top half of his tuxedo shirt was unbuttoned. And, last but not least- his New York accent was so thick you could slice it and put it on top of a piece of rye bread. Uh oh, everybody take cover – we have a real live Guido on our hands.

Now, in case you are not wise in the ways of such curious fleshly creatures, let me define for you the term Guido, via Wikipedia.com:

Guido (noun): slang term for a younger lower class or working class Italian-American. The Guido stereotype is often portrayed as humorously thuggish with an overtly macho attitude and an unyielding pride in his Italian ancestry.

I could not have worded that better. Oh Wikipedia, you never let me down.

I slowly retreated from the pre-matrimonial war zone to let the couple spend some "quality time" together before their big day began, hoping they wouldn't notice me leaving nor miss my absence. I didn't think the bride would need my assistance at that point. That, and I didn't want to be witness to a murder, so I quickly headed back downstairs.

A crowd was beginning to form outside the room where the ceremony was to be held. Complaints about the recent Yankee loss and a cluster of f-bombs could be heard throughout the air. I asked one guest which part of New York they were from.

"The Bronx, baby!" A fleck of his spit landed on my right cheek, and I could smell tobacco on his breath. He reached to give me a fist bump but I didn't reciprocate.

Now, I am sure there are many, many amazing, lovely people from the Bronx, but none of them were invited to this wedding.

The bickering couple managed to keep quiet and put on happy faces for the twenty-five minute ceremony. All their friends cheered and pumped their fists in the air as they exchanged their first kiss as a married couple, and with that – there was no turning back.

I headed to the kitchen to grab some bottles of wine and got ready to serve. When I emerged, my tables were already filled with guests. They were all men. They all had black hair and thick necks. They all had five o'clock shadows on their square, meaty faces. Five of them were wearing gold chains and two had fake diamond studs pierced through both of their lobes. They basically looked like the grooms' still-single counterparts, and I was completely terrified.

I approached the first guest to offer him wine. "Hello sir, would you care for some cabernet or pinot noir?"

"No, baby, but I would like a shot of Jaeger," he spat back, and let out a dry laugh as he banged his hand loudly on the table. He had something stuck in his right front tooth, and the stench of cigarettes he emitted formed a three-foot radius of repulsion around him. I weakly smiled at him, and moved on to the next guest.

"Wine, sir?" I asked. The man looked up and smiled. His teeth were poop-yellow. "Hey sugar, I like yo' gloves." He winked at me, beaming as if he had just given me a dozen roses. Was that a pickup line? I almost choked on the thick smell of his cologne. Was he wearing Cool Water? I hadn't smelled that since the seventh grade. Sigh. I knew it was going to be a long night. I poured him some red and moved on.

A man across the table waved his pudgy hand at me, gesturing me to walk over there. He had the menu in his hand, and was looking at it as if it was written in hieroglyphics.

"What is…fillot-mignony?" he asked me.

"It is steak, sir, and it is pronounced fillet mignon," I replied.

"I want something else," he said, then shoved the menu at me and turned away. Um…what is wrong with you, you spiky haired beast? Don't you know the deliciousness that is fillet mignon? Don't you realize that we servers risk our very livelihood just to sneak a few bites of its juicy goodness in the back kitchen freezer? This steak costs more than that gold chain hanging around your neck – eat the steak! But of course, being the superstar server I attempted to be, I just smiled and said, "Of course sir," and headed back into the kitchen.

Now, normally getting someone a meal substitute would not be an issue, but for some reason unknown to me, the bride specifically did not offer alternative dining options. Usually guests can easily exchange their meal for a vegetarian option, or for fish or chicken. I suppose this bride just assumed all of her guests would love tearing their chompers into a thick slab of bloody cow. But alas, one did not. So, I had to head all the way down to the basement kitchen and ask a chef to cook up a boring chicken concoction. The chef did it, but not before letting out a frustrated sigh and slamming down a pan a little too hard on the stove.

While this single chicken meal was cooking, I went back upstairs to serve the first course - a beet and goat cheese salad. None of the men at my tables ate it. I cleared the practically untouched plates and began serving the nine fillet mignons and one chicken dinner, which they promptly tore into like a pack of wolves. Ten minutes passed, and it was time for the wedding speeches to begin.

I didn't really give a speech at my wedding, except to say a quick and sincere thank you to everyone who joined us. I feel like this is what most brides do, leaving the big, heartfelt monologues to the maid of honor and best man. But tonight, first in line at the microphone was the bride herself. She stood in the center of the dance floor, her massively fluffy dress forming a five-foot radius around her.

"I just want to… " she began. She paused, as she already was starting to cry. "I just want to … sniff sniff, gwaaaaaaaaaaaaaaaaaaaaaaaaaa." Yes, that is the best way to spell out the sound that emerged from her mouth. Her shoulders began to shake, her mascara began to run, and a little snot gleamed in her right nostril. You know how some girls have a cute, pretty "crying face?" She was not one of those girls. She was moaning so loud that I thought humpback whales were going to jump out of the ocean and try to mate with her. For the next twenty minutes, she continued to proceed to alternate between barley decipherable words and the whale calls. Then, at minute twenty-four she loudly sniffled, caught her breath, and got real serious.

"I remember… guuuaaaaa sniff sniff… the first time… sniff whaaaaaaaaggggggrrr… I got high… sniff…with Benny…whaaaa… at summer camp."

Whoa. The blushing bride was fondly recounting her first moments of drug use in front of all her friends, family and loved ones at a wedding reception that probably cost over $200,000. Was this real life? Apparently it was, and she proceeded to go though other skanky memories from her glory years. The time she made out with Janet's boyfriend and never told her. The time she snuck liquor with the girls and got wasted in the high school bathroom. And the time she lost her virginity. Yes, she went there. Every topic that would be completely inappropriate for a wedding speech, she covered it. I was sure Great Grandpa Frankie loved hearing all these classy details.

At minute thirty-six of the speech, her father stood up from the table. I had seen him hit the bar several times earlier that night to get a refill on his whisky. I figured this was where he was headed again. However, he remained standing at the table for a good thirty seconds, slightly swaying back and forth. Just watching him was making me woozy. Then, he quickly turned around and ran for the exit, almost tripping over his chair on the way. He burst through the double doors to the outside patio, keeled over and vomited. Puking in the middle of your daughters wedding speech – amazing.

Craig ran to get some serious cleaning supplies, and the bride's brother also headed outside, at the time seemingly to help his father. He too was walking with a slight drunken swagger. He finally managed to make his way over to his dad, who was still on all fours awaiting another internal volcano eruption. The brother carefully bent over, his instability making me fear he was going to face plant in the puke pile. "Are you okay?" he slurred, then spewed right onto his dad's vomit pond. Like father, like son. In all my days working at the hotel I had never seen anyone loose their lunch from drinking too much, until that night, and it was a double feature - family style! The hotel should give them their own plaque for such an accomplishment. But the whale-noise-bride was unfazed by the gag fest happening outside, and continued on with her excruciating speech. Forty-eight[8] minutes into it she finally wrapped up, and loudly blew her nose as the crowd unenthusiastically clapped for her, many of their faces showing an expression of confusion. The only thing preventing me from throwing a rotten tomato at her head was the fact that I would probably have to clean it up afterward.

The rest of the night went as expected. The DJ played rap songs, and the guests fist-pumped their way onto the dance floor. Tuxedo jackets were removed, and the Guido men plucked open the top three buttons of their shirts to expose their sweaty tuffs of chest hair. Two more guests puked, the bar ran out of Jaeger, and the bride passed out on a table and got wedding cake in her hair. It was a perfect ending to a perfectly ridiculous wedding on the beautiful shores of Palm Beach, Florida.

---

[8] Forty-eight freaking minutes! Forty-eight! This far surpasses the acceptable time limit for any speech given, be it your wedding day or not. Granted, half of it was in humpback language – but being bi-lingual does not disqualify you from the rules.

The Silver Haired Seductress

I am just going to be blunt. My husband is handsome. I know I might be a little biased, but it is true - he is a stud. I am eternally grateful that by the end of high school his prepubescent acne cleared up and his jaw grew to be masculine and strong. He has blue eyes and wears his dishwater blonde hair perfectly tousled. He played football in high school, but then discovered he really is an artist at heart, can sing Frank Sinatra perfectly, and is an amazing actor. And, I love him. Which is good because we are married, and despite what Hollywood tells me, I still believe love should fall into that equation somewhere.

People are always noticing and commenting on how cute he is, especially older women. Cougar-aged women always like him, and can sometimes be a little too expressive of those feelings. For example, when he was a high school pizza delivery boy (everyone loves a man in uniform), a middle-ager once answered the door and received her pie dressed in just her bra and mom jeans. She smiled at him seductively as she pulled the greasy pepperoni and cheese delectableness from his hands, and made sure to give him a hefty tip. So, so weird. You can kind of get the picture - old and young women swoon for his Prince Charming good looks. But one evening at work, the particular woman who was smitten with my man fell way past the age limit of "cougar." Perhaps a better animal representation would be an elephant, or tortoise? I don't know, whatever you call ladies on the prowl that also qualify for senior discounts at restaurants.

Kyle was making the rounds at his tables, offering drinks and lapping napkins, when this cute, seemingly innocent grandma creature beckoned to him with her knobby wrinkled fingers. She had something to tell him, and it looked important.

Would she like a Coke? Vodka tonic? Caviar beggars pouch with crème fresh? Oh no, this g-master funk wanted much, much more than mere refreshments.

She pulled Kyle in close, so close he could smell the Fixodent on her breath. She whispered into his ear, her frail voice just loud enough to be heard over the band and crowd chatter. "If I was fifty years younger, I would take you upstairs and put your boots under my bed." Kyle tilted his head at hearing such a forward statement, his eyes widening in surprise.

Although the saying 'I want to put your boots under my bed' was not something that the posh, hip, perfect-bodied American youth typically threw around when they were looking for a little lovin'— Kyle got the picture. He politely declined the elephant's advances and continued his serving duties, a slight expression of bewilderment and terror remaining on his face.

The night rolled along, and try as he may to avoid the Erotic Elder who wanted to get it on like Donkey Kong, Kyle had to bring her dinner. That involved leaning over her and plopping down a heavy ceramic plate piled with steak and vegetables – both a consistency the woman's dentures likely could not successfully chew, God bless her for trying. Kyle attempted to set the plate down with extreme precision. The table was crowded, and he was trying extremely hard to avoid all physical contact with the woman without spilling the dinner in her lap in the process. Just when the plate hit the table, she quickly reached out and grabbed his wrist, her knobby digits wrapping firm around his arm as if driven by some unseen force. Kyle was momentarily taken aback by her unusual strength, and stared at her like a poor, helpless dear caught in a headlight of unwanted desire. The silver-haired seductress brought his hand up to her face, looked deep into his eyes, and licked his palm.

At the first feel of saliva, Kyle yanked his arm back in sheer terror. He glanced around to see if anyone has witnessed this odd debauchery, but everyone was too engrossed with scarfing their slabs of dead cow to notice. Kyle quickly turned to walk away, making a beeline to the kitchen so he could wash the old lady saliva off of his hand, shuddering in disgust.

Just when he thought he was safe and it would soon turn into a terrible distant memory, he heard a voice calling out, "Wait! Wait! Come back, handsome!" The passionate poligrip had gotten out of her chair and was shuffling after Kyle in her sparkly blue loafers, a feeble yet gallant attempt at capturing her one true love. A small cry of horror escaped Kyle's lips at the sight. He hurried into kitchen and slammed the door shut behind him, leaning up against it just to be sure the wrinkled-hip-wiggler didn't bust in.

It was then that I emerged from the kitchen's cooler, after just downing two Diet Cokes with perfect server stealth. Kyle looked as if he had seen a ghost, which was probable since we both were avid watchers of the SyFy show Ghost Hunters and we knew exactly what to look for.

"What happened? Did you see the billowing spirit of Michael Jackson? Did he dance for you?" I asked. If I could see the ghost of anybody, I think Michael Jackson would be the most entertaining, and likely the most frightening.

He explained the whole situation with the white haired wonder, and I laughed so hard some of my Diet Coke resurfaced into my nose.

"She CHASED you?" I snorted. But Kyle did not think it was as humorous, and he went into the cooler to stuff a chocolate chip cookie down his throat to numb his feelings.

Being the loving wife that I was, I took over his table the rest of the night so he could avoid any other terrifying confrontations that involved another human being's spit. Each time I would pass the desiring dinosaur, it took all I had in me not to fall over laughing again. Her eyes scanned the ballroom every few minutes, clearly looking for her long lost love. But Kyle had resorted to sitting in the kitchen filling up saltshakers, sweeping, or doing absolutely anything possible to avoid going back into the ballroom to face his ninety-year-old seductress. That woman was in desperate need of a cold shower. And probably some prune juice, because I think old people like that or something.

Delicacies of Desperation

The story of the tired, frustrated waiter is nothing new. The job can be difficult and exhausting, both physically and mentally. When you show up at the hotel you never know if you are going to be working for a few hours, or until three in the morning. You never know if you are going to get a two-hour dinner break, or none at all. I sometimes wondered how labor laws played into this scenario, but I didn't have enough time to think about it as I was running down the hallway to fetch a forgotten plated dinner before a guest threw a fit over their delayed dining experience.

I have written about several of my sneaky snacking adventures at the hotel, risking my job for a decadent treat in the kitchen freezer, or behind a stack of chairs. However, some nights there are just no extra hors d'oeuvres lying around, no dinners to devour, no leftover cheesecake to thicken my thighs with or even a renegade dinner roll to quiet my hunger pains. Some nights the back kitchen is as desolate as the wide African plains during the dry season, not a morsel of food or nutrients in sight. As I write this, I picture tumbleweeds blowing by all of us exhausted and starving servers as we lay on the ground, too weak from our foodless shift to continue living.

This, of course, is a slightly dramatic description. However, there have been many shifts where eight hours go by, and I have yet to find time to use the restroom let alone find something to eat. One particular foodless night a fellow server, completely fed up and irrational from starvation, went to desperate measures to fill the aching hollowness of his empty gut.

The shift began at 4:30 in the afternoon. I lazily clocked in and made my way up to the ballroom where the event was to be held. It was a fundraiser for a charity that provided food for struggling families in South Florida. How ironic.

Craig was standing in the center of the room, a gaggle of tuxedo-wearing bandits gathered around him as he gave the rundown for the evening.

"Listen up everyone, it is 4:40 right now. In exactly one hour we need to have this entire room set up, and be over at the reception ready to pass wine. The contact moved the party up an hour, so we don't have a lot of time. Get to work!"

Just as he was finishing, an employee wheeled in a large cart full of silverware that we were to sort, polish, and place neatly on our tables in now less than one hour. For some reason that I never really understood, silverware instantly changed my coworkers from respectable, tux-wearing comrades into savage beasts who will stop at nothing to get the correct amount of forks for their table.

We all made a mad dash to the cart, and began shoving and sorting our way through the piles of utensils, still warm and damp from the dishwasher. The sound of shouting and clanking metal was loud, and I got my foot stepped on by Amos, the elderly silverware-polishing Ninja who has no mercy when it comes to getting his tables set up. He offered no apology, and we continued ransacking the utensils as if the mere number we were able to snag constituted our worth as a human being. I managed to grab the last fourteen salad knives, six short of what my tables required. Drat! Luckily, I got the correct twenty salad and twenty dinner forks, and corresponding spoons and entree knives. I headed to my tables to set up. I would have to go on a hunt for those six extra knives later – no time to worry about them now.

This pre-shift chaos was far too common, something we all had become accustomed to, yet still despised. Why we have to turn into Neanderthals just to set our tables, I will never understand. I worked quickly and was making sure everything was perfectly aligned when Craig began yelling, "Five more minutes, five more minutes!" about every ten minutes or so, until there actually really was only five minutes left. At that point, I began walking around the room to see if anybody had extra salad knives I could take to complete my set. I approached Amos, my toes still hurting from when he stomped on them earlier. He had ten extra knives, that son-of-a-B. I pleaded with him until he finally gave in and handed me the six I needed to complete my set, but not without scowling at me first and mumbling something that sounded like a curse at me.

With my tables finally completed, I hurried over to the reception to begin my evening of servitude. I walked into the back kitchen to pick up some food to pass, but instead saw just tables with glasses of champagne and sparkling water with lime slices.

"Are there any hors d'oeuvres?" I asked Craig, hoping with all my might there was an abundance hiding in the fridge just waiting to be served.[9]

"No, the contact just wanted to pass drinks. Take this." He handed me a silver tray with eight champagne glasses on it. It was really heavy, and with every step the slender glasses teetered and rattled against each other. If I sneezed, they would have all blown over like daisies in a tornado and crashed into a mess of glass, alcohol and stickiness. I was not even at the ballroom yet and my arm was already aching under the weight. My stomach let out its first hunger grumble of the evening.

Two hours later, the reception finally finished. My arm felt like a dead eel, exhausted and limp from passing endless amounts of bubbly beverages. I went back into the kitchen where my friend Ken was gulping down a Dr. Pepper in an attempt to put some calories into his body. I pulled out the menu to see what we would be serving for the evening.

"Sweet. The first course is a goat cheese and arugula salad, my favorite!"

---

[9] And by served I mean eaten by me in a shadowy corner.

Ken had already opened his second soda. "I freaking love goat cheese," he said, as a little brown liquid dripped from the corner of his mouth. "I would bathe in goat cheese if I had the chance."

That statement was a little extreme, but at that point, I was so starving that a bathtub of goat cheese did sound appealing.

Ken and I headed to the ballroom to begin pouring wine and passing around the first course. About twenty minutes later, it was time to clear. I loaded the half eaten salads onto a tray and carried them into the back. Ken was there, holding a plate over the garbage can, inspecting it with fervor.

"What are you doing?" I asked, already creeped out by his bathtub comment earlier.

"I don't think this person even touched their salad," he said, his eyes wide with desire.

"Ken, don't do it." I have never been the type of server to eat off a guest's plate. Who knows what kind of fungal diseases they may have growing on their crusty lips? Disgusting.

"I don't know, I think it looks fine," he said, and he licked his lips. He brought the plate closer to his face for further examination. Just as he did, the delicious herbed covered hunk of cheese rolled off of the plate, onto the floor, and under the counter.

"Noooooo!" Ken yelled, as if he had just lost his first-born child. The hunger was making him completely irrational.

"Let it go, Ken, let it go," I said, trying to console him. He sighed and dumped the rest of the salad in to the garbage. Without the goat cheese it lost all value. We headed back into the ballroom to continue our slavery, our stomachs growling in beat with the band.

The main course was served – panko-crusted halibut with a delicious cream sauce on a bed of garlic mashed potatoes. There were none left over for the servers to steal, duh. The dessert was then passed – chocolate molten lava cake with vanilla ice cream and caramel sauce. Again, no leftovers. Whoever planned this party was apparently meticulous about saving money. No hors d'oeuvres at the reception, and the exact number of meals to be served. Usually at parties there was enough food left over to feed every homeless person in three counties. That night, the kitchen looked like it was attacked by a clan of rabid obese people who ransacked it for every morsel of food possible. There was nothing to eat. Nothing.

After I cleared dessert, I headed back into the kitchen to get a soda, finally coming to terms with my foodless fate for the evening.

When I got back there, Ken was on his hands and knees, reaching under the stainless steel counter to get his renegade chunk of goat cheese he had dropped there over an hour ago.

"Ken! What are you doing! Don't, please don't." But my cries did no good - Ken was hungry and desperate. The only thing available to satisfy him was that dust-covered cheese ball. He looked at me, looked at the warm goat cheese now resting in his palm. He picked a hair off of it, popped it in his mouth, and swallowed.

I covered my mouth and almost gagged. This had to have been an all time server low – the sickest of all sick waiter eats.

"Ken! Taking food off of a half eaten tray is one thing, but freaking eating old cheese from under a counter where the mop can't reach…seriously?"

But Ken was too busy savoring the creamy herb and kitchen sludge covered cheese to care. He had crossed a dark line that could never be undone. He had the job take a part of his dignity, and he could never get that back. Actually it was really not that serious- I just felt like making a super dramatic statement. It was just super, super disgusting and Ken probably should have considered getting an antibiotic. But in spite of my disgust, I could kind of understand where Ken was coming from. Extreme hunger can make human beings do funny things. At least he didn't go all Hannibal Lecter on us.

The Money You Spent on a Cake Could Feed An African Village For a Year - This Angers Me

Every year around summertime and into the fall, there is a lull in shifts that carves a big empty space into my bank account. This year, Kyle and I especially noticed this "dry season" of work, since we were in the middle of America's new favorite friend: The Recession. Oh Mr. Recession, I loathe you more than math, greasy possums and having to buy my own healthcare combined. Please die.

But it was not just we college kids affected by this obnoxious economic downturn. Many people who we relied on for business were scaling back in their extravagant Palm Beach spending. There were far less private parties being held at the hotel than usual and several companies had to cancel their big fancy conventions at the last minute, taking big chunks out of our work schedules. Not to mention Bernie Madoff, who "made off" with several Palm Beachers' money, so even some socialites were feeling it.[10]

But seriously, the recession sucked. However, despite times being a little financially tight, I would continually thank God I even had a job at all, when so many Americans were without, even if said job requires me to dress in drag. There is no

---

[10] That joke never gets old to me, despite its cheesiness and complete lack of originality. I mean come on, could he have had a more appropriate last name? It is almost as good as my middle school art teacher being named Art. Seriously I can't make crap like that up. His name was Art. I can't handle it.

difference between a woman in a tux and necktie and a man in a dress. None.

Anyway, it really was surreal working in an environment of such excessive wealth when almost everyone else, myself included, seemed to be struggling financially. All I have is a growing credit card bill, while the women I am serving are carrying around these weird little rhinestone purses in the shape of stupid things like cupcakes and polar bears. I Googled those sparkly pieces of tackiness once – they cost thousands of dollars. That is wrong on so many levels. I constantly have to fight against my bitterness.

On one particular night, I had just about had it with Palm Beach, and my resentment won the battle. I showed up at work to learn we were going to work a wedding. Weddings are generally pretty good shifts to have, at least ones not overridden by Guidos. The majority of wedding guests are usually cheerful relatives flown in from some nondescript Midwest town who are just happy to be getting a free meal and view of the ocean.

This shift's wedding reception seemed to be even more stunning and extravagant than most. It was in our biggest ballroom, which can easily hold a thousand people. It was so exceedingly decorated I could barely recognize it. A huge stage was set up in front and a twelve piece band had already started warming up for their long evening of providing background music for people to embarrass themselves while on the dance floor. White linen hung floor to ceiling on every wall, covering up the gaudy floral wallpaper and making it seem like we were in a fairy tale. Four-foot tall flower arrangements with long, winding sprigs of willow sat on every table, with delicate crystals hanging from the branches. The tablecloths were silver, and the plates and cups were crystal clear with metallic decorative edging. There were bars in every corner of the room, and near the back was a massive candy buffet that would have made Willy Wonka jealous.

But no wedding would be complete without a cake. That night's celebratory pastry sat in the back under its own spotlight, illuminated in a way that I felt we should bow down and worship it. It was five tiers tall, and would have easily towered over a small midget. It had intricate white flowers covering its entirety, all made completely out of sugar. But despite all the sugary glory, I was not that impressed. I have seen way better cake creations in my day. I know someone whose wedding cake was shaped like the head of Darth Vader. Now that was something to gawk over, not a simple, white cake covered in edible flowers. And besides, I had tasted those flowers before, and a can of Betty Crocker frosting trumps them any day. They taste like sweet, chewy cardboard. Bon appetit!

I was standing there examining and silently critiquing the cake when Craig came over. In his thick, Indian accent he muttered, "She's a beauty, isn't she?" Until that point I was always unsure of what gender to classify cake, but now I knew.

"She was flown in from New York this morning on a private jet. This little baby costs more than that ugly Toyota you drive."

I stared at him, my brow scrunched together in annoyance. I decided to just ignore his statement about my car, which I happen to love. Craig was known for saying weird, half rude comments, and was also missing a tooth, so I couldn't take anything he said too seriously. But even though he dissed my hot wheels, I was still intrigued by the knowledge he possessed about this massive cake. I decided to pry it from him out of my sheer boredom and lack of anything better to do.

"How much did it cost, Craig?"

"Well… I shouldn't say." But his shifty eyes, raised brows and quick examination of his fingernails said otherwise.

"Craig, tell me. You must. If you don't, I'll tell your father you eat steak every night after your shift."

Craig is Hindu, a religion whose followers don't typically eat beef, unless they are Craig. He ate it more than he drank water. His precious seventy-two year old dad works as a dishwasher in the basement, and I knew he would be absolutely horrified if I told him how many cows Craig consumed on a regular basis.

"Okay, fine, I will tell you. But you must never tell my father about the steak or he will drown me in his dirty dishwater. The cake costs…" He grabbed my shoulders firmly and got way too close to my face, breaking my personal space bubble, as he was known to do. His breath smelled like cigarettes. "It cost fifty thousand dollars. Now do not tell a soul!" He turned and hustled back into the kitchen, looking over his shoulder as if the wedding police were hot on his trail.

I just about choked on my gum upon hearing such epic ludicrousness. Fifty freaking thousand dollars? You have got to be kidding me. The cake suddenly turned into a living entity that I had a huge distaste for. It became a person I envied no matter how hard I tried not to. A person I wanted to talk badly about at work even though I knew it was wrong. It became a person driving a Porsche who just cut me off in traffic while I putted along in my little Toyota. You get the picture. I hated that cake.

But as fate would have it, my tables were stationed right next to the pastry shrine, so it could sit there and mock me as I shuffled around in my K-mart loafers. One freaking slice of that thing could pay my car payment. The whole thing could provide an African village with clean drinking water, or fund someone's entire college education. This angers me.

The evening went on and as the cake sat looming over me, I realized I was glaring at it out of spite. This was a new low point of my life - I was glaring at a pastry. I needed to get a new job. We served the three-course meal: an arugula and Gorgonzola salad to start, herb grilled filet mignon and grilled veggies in a tiny skillet for the main course and the ever so delicious martini sundae for dessert. It was vanilla ice cream and warm chocolate chip cookies in a massive martini glass the size of a human face, with tiny waffle cups filled with candy and toppings to pile on top. Then we, the servers, passed around hot fudge and caramel sauce from dainty silver bowls. It was by far the most delicious sundae I had ever consumed. I didn't even want to know how many calories they were because I have been known to eat two in one evening.

After we served dessert, the moment I had been waiting for all night finally arrived. It was time for that $50,000 sugary mound to go under the knife. Craig carefully wheeled the pastry into the back. I held my breath as he did so, half hoping he would trip and the cake would see its demise. But to my disappointment, Craig made it safely into the kitchen, got a knife and began the slicing and dicing. I wanted to take the first stab at that delicious waste of money, but I probably would have mutilated it out of rage rather then cut nice, neat pieces.

Craig divided up the pieces and put them on small plates, which we then loaded up on trays and brought back in to the ballroom. I began passing it around the table, but half of the people declined. I looked around the room and noticed most of the servers still had full trays of the cake. It appeared that very few guests had enough caloric ambition left to squeeze in a slice. It says a lot when Americans are even too full for a piece of cake, especially one that is comparable in price to six acres of land in rural Kentucky. Who could blame them, as they literally just ate two full courses, then a sundae bigger than their face? No one should have had any room left in their guts to spare.

We take our rejected cake back into the kitchen, and asked Craig what to do with it. Since the night was wrapping up and guests were starting to trickle out, he just shrugged his shoulders and said, "Toss it."

Um…wow. That cake may qualify as the biggest waste of money in the nation's history, after the Christmas decorations the White House puts up every year, of course. I picked up a plate and dumped a piece into the garbage can. And with each piece that made a soft thump against the bottom of the trash, I added up how much money I was tossing away like a used Kleenex. $100, $200, $300 worth of cake gone in less than a minute. Disgusting.

Finally, when about $45,000 worth of cake was piled in the trash cans, I returned to the ballroom to finish clearing renegade dirty dishes and empty wine glasses. My tables had been near the bride's family all night, and it was quite obvious that post-cake time her father was not in the best mood. He sat at his table with his arms crossed, a scowl on his face, muttering to himself under his breath. As the night wrapped up and the band quieted, I could hear him grumbling complaints to whoever would listen as I plucked the remaining dirty napkins from his table.

"I can't believe I spent $50,000 on a cake nobody ate," he said to his wife, who was trying with no avail to cheer him up. "We should have just gone to COSTCO," he said as he threw his arms up in the air in frustration.

I have to admit, I ate a piece of that cake before I dumped it all in the trash, as I am sure anyone would, just out of sheer curiosity as to what a $50,000 cake tasted like. With a price tag that high the cake should have made me lose weight and my boobs grow bigger, but of course it did not.[11] However, it was delicious, as one would expect a cake the price of a show horse would taste. Each slice had five layers, and between each was a different flavored filling: vanilla, chocolate, strawberry, and lemon. The cake was so moist I could have rung it out and showered under its sweet nectar. It was good. Really good. But the disgruntled father of the bride had a point. Costco cake is also delicious. In fact, Costco cake is so delicious it makes me want to break out in a tap dance routine. So here's to you, Costco, for keeping America fed at reasonable prices. I will take a slice of your cake over that five-tier pretentiousness any day. And besides, you can get a picture printed on Costco cakes, and that is just plain cool.

---

[11] Neither did those pills I bought off of the Home Shopping Channel.

Attack of the Nude

There is a cute Haitian man who works at the hotel, named Peter. He is about five feet tall, and has the most joy-inducing accent ever. He frequently takes out a picture of his two-year-old baby boy and talks about him with great pride, as any good father should. Peter always has an almost-mustache growing above his top lip. It looks like the mustache that a fifteen year old boy who hasn't yet discovered how to use a razor would have - a few splotchy patches of hair and nothing much else. But Peter is not fifteen; he is a full-grown man, a father, and a hard worker. He sings in the church choir every Sunday, and taught me how to call people ugly in Creole. I use the phrase often, and Peter bends over laughing whenever I do. Peter is adorable, Peter is nice, and Peter is awesome. Poor, poor Peter. No, he did not die, you morbid little creature, but he experienced one of the most terrible things a waiter could ever experience. Worse than having the rudest guest of all time. Worse than not getting tipped by ten tables in a row. Much, much worse.

Peter was assigned to work a small event one evening. It was a birthday party for a forty-something-year-old hotshot lawyer who wore expensive-looking pointy leather dress shoes and a pea-green tie spotted with tiny white embroidered whales. His black hair was slicked to the side, and he wore thick, tortoise shell-rimmed glasses, his retro-looking yet stylish accessories making him resemble an old school Clark Kent, minus the handsome, mysterious charm and ability to save the world. He had massive teeth, obviously veneers, that were stained around the edges from sucking in too much nicotine. His skin was tan, but the carroty tint indicated it was a spray on. He had rented out one of our small ballrooms for the evening. In the back left corner was a two-person reggae band, one man on keyboard and one on steel drum. This reggae duo is used often at the hotel, much to my delight. Both musicians have long gray dreads that reach the back of their thighs, tons of laugh lines around their aging faces and they can play any Bob Marley hit known to man. For that reason alone, I love them.

In the middle of the room were three long tables covered with shimmering silver linens. Each was topped with blue base plates, white flower arrangements, and a dozen or so different sized antique silver candlesticks casting a romantic light. Since there were only about fifteen guests, Peter was the only server working this party. Kyle and I, along with a dozen or so other tuxedo bandits, were across the hall in our largest ballroom, working some ho-hum corporate event. The guests at my function were all wearing slightly wrinkled business suits and had a constant look of stress on their faces, no matter how much whisky was served. Boring.

Peter was told to pass champagne as the guests arrived. He stood near the door with a tray filled with glasses of Cristal - only the best for the hotshot lawyer. As people arrived, the tray cleared quickly. Peter had to go back into the kitchen four times within the first half hour to get more, opening bottle after bottle of the expensive bubbly. Kyle and I were in the back of the kitchen during one of Peter's fill up sessions. Kyle was telling me about one of his guests that had just farted, right as he was handing him a pig in a blanket. After passing gas, the elderly man looked at Kyle, shrugged, ate the tiny hot dog and walked away, leaving a cloud of foul smelling doom behind him. I was laughing so hard I was bent over like an old woman who forgot to take her calcium pills for the last thirty years, and I was throwing down an "awkward turtle" hand motion when Peter arrived.

"What are you doing with your hands?" he asked, as he began pulling the gold foil off of another bottle of champagne.

"It's the awkward turtle," I explained when I had calmed down enough to get coherent words out.

"Awkward... turtle?" Peter asked, his face scrunched in confusion.

Now, dear reader, snuggle up for a life changing lesson on "The Awkward Turtle." It is a hand gesture fondly used by my close group of college friends, but I encourage all to partake it its life changing ways. To make the awkward turtle, place one hand on top of the other, and wiggle around your thumbs, thus creating something that resembles a discomfited turtle. When something extremely uncomfortable happens, we make the hand motion to announce to the world that this is an extremely awkward moment. Sometimes it can be used to break the tension of a situation, and sometimes it can be done in secret to show a nearby friend that the person you are talking to has a massive piece of lettuce stuck in their front teeth and will not stop talking about their Pokémon obsession.

Here are some excellent examples as to when the awkward turtle would be completely appropriate:

Example 1: Setting: Valentine's Day, at a very expensive restaurant you can't really afford. You have been dating this girl for a couple months, and falling head over heels for her. What better day to express your devotion then today?

Boy: "I think I am in love with you."
Girl: "That's ... sweet. Excuse me, I have to go to the bathroom." And she hurries away.
Boy: Does the "Awkward turtle" hand motion subtly under the table.

Example 2: Setting: The office, right after the lunch hour. It is very quiet as people delve back into their workload.

That weird co-worker who doesn't really have a sense of humor lets out an extremely loud and long fart. Everyone hears it, and then smells it. But nobody says anything, they just keep typing away as if nothing ever happened. Cue: The awkward turtle hand motion under your desk.

Example 3: Setting: The office again.

You just got a new boss at work. You dressed extra professionally that day, as you wanted to make a good first impression. He spots you across the room and approaches you to introduce himself. You look up and him, give your best professional butt-kissing smile, and then realize he has a ridiculous lazy eye. I mean, really ridiculous. Where do you look? The right eye, the left? Your good first impression is thrown off by you trying to pretend he does not have an eye all out of wack, and you end up glancing down at the papers you are holding as if they actually contained some important information. After he walks away, Cue: Awkward turtle to your co-worker in the next cubicle.

As I explain all this to Peter, he bends over laughing like a crotchety old lady with osteoporosis, then scurries back into the party to continue serving. That is what is so great about Peter – you say one semi-funny thing and he makes you feel like Jerry Seinfeld on his best night.

As he re-entered the ballroom, he noticed the lawyer was in the middle of the room surrounded by a gaggle of friends, and he had a blonde-haired, big-chested woman linked to his arm. Her dress was so short it looked like it was made out of the same silver cloth napkins resting on the table. The lawyer spotted Peter, and made an obnoxiously large hand motion to beckon him over.

"Happy birthday, sir," Peters said. "What can I get for you?"

"What's your name, kid?" the man asked, even though Peter is thirty-six years old and anything but a child. Maybe the almost-mustache threw him off.

"Peter, sir," he replied.

"Great, Paul, nice to meet you. Get a round of Jaeger shots for the whole room, please." The lawyer turned his back on him before he could correct him on his name. Peter just sighed and walked to the bar set up in the corner of the room. He got fifteen shots from the bartender, loaded them on the tray, and began passing them out to the crowd. The lawyer picked up a fork from a table and clinked it on the side of his glass.

"Ladies and gentlemen, my co-workers, my friends, even you, Paul… " the hot shot lawyer began, flashing his large teeth to the crowd. "I want to thank you all for coming out tonight. Now let's have one hell of a good time. Cheers!" He raised his shot glass in the air. The rest of the room said cheers, and they all took the Jaeger shots with the precision and grace of a group of frat boys.

"Another round!" the lawyer shouted, and Peter headed back to the bar.

The night continued on. Dinner was served, but the guests were far less interested in the five-course meal placed before them than they were with the open bar. Peter was running back and forth getting drink, after drink, after drink. At about 11:00, the party moved outside to the beach. The lawyer had arranged for a bonfire to be lit right in the sand, where they would finish up the night next to the crashing waves. There was a buffet table of desserts set up: key lime pie on a stick, cheesecake lollipops, and a birthday cake in the shape of a topless mermaid. There were tiki torches lit and music was blaring out of speakers disguised as big rocks. There was also a coffee bar set up, and Peter had hoped that he would be done serving drinks for the night, as the guests would switch to the caffeinated liquid in an attempt to sober up some. He was wrong. "Pauull," the lawyer slurred, "a rum and coke please."

"Yes sir. Can I get anybody else something from the bar?" he asked the group, which had by that point slimmed down to about seven guests. Nobody responded, so Peter went back inside to get the drink. When he returned to the beach, the lawyer's date was sitting on his lap, and she had removed her shoes.

"Margarita, please!" she said to Peter, and threw her head back in drunken laughter for no apparent reason.

"Yes, ma'am," he replied as he handed the lawyer a drink. "Can I get anybody else something from the bar?" Again, nobody responded. He headed back into the hotel, got the margarita, returned to the beach and handed it to the blonde.

Another woman, with an unsettlingly tall bouffant of a hairdo and dress a so sparkly it looked like a Care Bear threw up on it, saw the drink. "Is that a margarita? Yummm! I'll take one!"

"Yes ma'am, of course. Anybody ELSE?" Peter said, four decibels louder than his last two offers. Again, nobody responded, all still engrossed in their drunken conversations.

He went back inside again to get the margarita, returned to the beach, and handed it to the woman. The crowd was now a group of five. The remaining two drink-less people saw the beverage and said "margaritas!" as if this were a new concept. "We want one!"

Peter sighed, loudly enough for the guests to hear him, and headed back inside for the fourth time. Kyle and I were cleaning up some broken glass in the hall when Peter walked by with his head hung low. He explained about his drink order runaround, and I completely sympathized. Why do people do this to us servers? Please, everybody, order your drinks at the same time and the world will become a better place filled with nicer servers, beautiful rainbows and a surplus of purring kittens.

Peter got the two additional margaritas and trudged back outside. As he neared the beach, he could tell the party had significantly quieted down, which struck him as odd. He arrived at the bonfire to discover that everyone had left, leaving their drinks scattered about, barely even sipped on. He could hear some laughter farther down the beach and figured they must have gone for a walk.

Frustrated, Peter began cleaning up the disgraceful mess they had all left behind when he heard a rustling coming from behind some palm trees. He squinted his eyes, trying to see into the darkness, when a person stepped out into the light cast by the still burning fire. It was the lawyer's blonde girlfriend. She was completely naked. Peter dropped his tray into the sand and let out a yelp.

"Paul," she said, and she started slowly walking towards him. Peter quickly turned and headed back towards the hotel, completely terrified. "Wait, Paul, I don't want a margarita, I want youuuuu! Don't you want me back?" She began running after him. Peter heard her let out a little cry, and he glanced back over his shoulder to see that in her drunkenness she had tripped and face-planted into the sand. Peter hurried into the hotel and burst into the kitchen, where Kyle and I were tidying up the final remnants from our party. He looked horrified.

"Peter, are you okay? What happened?" I asked, thinking perhaps he had seen a ghost of Palm Beach past. He put his butt against the wall and slid it down to the floor so he was sitting in a defeated looking slump. He looked up at Kyle and I, lifted one hand, then placed the other on top of it, and began wiggling his thumbs.

"Awkward... turtle," he said, still out of breath. As he explained the entire situation to us, I tried to stifle my chuckles out of respect for poor Peter, with little success. Despite the hilarity and immense awkwardness of the situation, I mostly felt bad for him. Nobody should have to be chased on a lonely beach by a nude socialite, her blonde hair extensions flying in the wind behind her like crazed Medusa. We agreed to go back out to the fire to help Peter clean up, promising to ward off any naked demons that may come flying at him.

Luckily for all of us, by the time we got back out there the entire party had packed up and left, leaving behind only their untouched drinks and the naked blonde's shoes. At least she didn't leave behind her dress. Although seeing people walking about Palm Beach scantily clad is a regular occurrence, I don't think walking around buck naked would have been received with the same leniency. Poor, poor Peter. Awkward turtle, indeed.

I Eat Lip Gloss For Breakfast

Every woman in the world dreams of a situation like the one I am about to tell you about. Well, I suppose there are some who could care less, but those are more the types of women who get Justin Bieber haircuts and have a strong affection towards sports bras.

CoCo was rocking the tuxedo with me one fateful waitress evening. We were working outside, sweaty and frizzy-haired from the Florida heat. We were halfway through a weeklong convention that comes every year to the hotel. All the big shot cosmetic companies that stock the shelves of drug stores gather to show off their merchandise. Every major brand of beauty product is represented. The whole week is one big self-promoting, networking, show-off fest. At least that is how they describe it in the program. All the product reps try to get the different drug stores to buy their goods. They mostly try and promote their products by throwing insane, overly priced banquets for the buyers, a shameless attempt to win their love and financial devotion. Huge ballrooms with Cirque du Soleil performances, concerts from famous singers, or fashion shows usually set the bar for minimum spectacle required to get noticed. This year we had Jewel and Seal perform. I guess the theme was 90's singers with one name. Madonna must have been busy.

CoCo was being extra chatty with the guests that evening, most likely in the hopes of scoring a big tip. CoCo could flat out tell someone they were ugly and had B.O. and they would still tip her. She has lucky dust farts coming out of her at every moment, putting everyone around her in a magical spell that makes them just want to give her money. She is blessed like that. A man once tipped her $200 for getting him three drinks. I'm not bitter. Okay, I am a little bitter.

Anyway, she was spreading her magical dust all around the room that evening, and one particular guest fell prey to her spell. While refilling the woman's water glass and making polite small talk, the woman said, "You know, you look like Sarah Michelle Gellar."[12]

"Thanks!" CoCo said. "I get that a lot actually."

"Yeah? That is so funny. I'm Susan," the woman said, and reached out to shake CoCo's gloved hand. Susan had wavy, sandy blonde hair and a small gold hoop through her left nostril. She looked like the perfect mix of movie star glam and dirty hippy. I would assume she used a lot of organic makeup and participated in early morning yoga workouts on the beach.

The pair chatted for a while, and eventually it came up that Susan was a makeup artist, and she had been doing makeovers all weekend for convention goers.

"Do you want to swing by my booth tomorrow and I can do your makeup before your shift?" she asked. Um… yes please! Coco said of course, and they arranged a time to meet.

The next day, CoCo arrived an hour before her shift began. She went to the back of the hotel to a small conference room where Susan said to meet her. CoCo opened the heavy wooden door, peeked in, and almost peed her pants in excitement. No, she did not see a naked Bear Grylls filming a "how to survive Palm Beach" episode, rather something much better.[13] What she saw was an entire room packed full of free makeup samples. Table after table was set up with mounds of Covergirl, Revlon, Neutrogena - basically everything a girl could ever want. Nail polish, face powder, blush, eyeliner and lip-gloss

---

[12] Bet you weren't expecting to see that name in this book. Sarah Michelle, where are you these days? Attempting to slay the vampires from Twilight most likely.

[13] Well, kind of better. Bear Grylls is amazingly adorable. It's a toss up.

of every shade was sitting in piles, free for the taking. Once CoCo managed to close her gaping mouth and wipe the saliva off her chin, she walked over to where Susan was setting up. She sat CoCo down in the chair and began the makeover. Light chitchat was exchanged while they got down to business. CoCo explained how she became a tuxedo-wearing waitress, and Susan revealed her undying love for sushi. A dabble of rouge, a brush of mascara and a poof of face powder later, Susan pulled back and smiled.

"Finished!"

Coco glanced in the mirror – she looked magazine cover ready. Well, I suppose if the magazine was Tuxedo Monthly. Despite her ugly outfit, her makeup looked flawless.

"You look great!" Susan said.

She paused here for a moment as she stared at Coco. The room was so quiet you can hear the ocean waves crashing outside. Susan closed her perfectly painted eyes, lifted her arms up in the air and asked, "Can I pray for you?"

That was not what Coco expected. I mean, we are both big fans of a little shout out to the Lord, but this one came out of left field. "Sure?" CoCo replied, as she hesitantly bowed her newly made-up face, keeping one eye slightly cracked open to assess the situation.

"Oh, Mother Earth, oh spirit winds. Oh, pretty little birds flying in the sky… " Susan began, and she started waving her hands in the hair and spinning in a circle. This was by far the most unique prayer CoCo had ever heard, a far stretch from those at our non-denominational church downtown. Susan wrapped up by asking the nature world to shower blessings upon CoCo. It was a terribly strange yet somewhat lovely experience. But mostly just strange. CoCo politely said thank you, and got up to leave when Susan stopped her. Another prayer? Nope, this time a miracle.

"Oh! Before you go, take this bag. Go around the room and take whatever you want," said spiritual-makeup-slinger Susan.

CoCo quietly gasped, took the bag, and glanced around the room, her brown eyes wide with cosmetic desire. She casually walked up to a table and examined the goods, deciding what to take. She played it cool for about twenty seconds before she thought 'screw it,' put off her dignified front and let her animalistic instincts reign. She started shoving loads and loads of makeup into the bag, looking like a homeless woman at an unattended hot dog stand. At one point she tripped in her excitement, fell to the ground, got right back up and kept piling stuff into her bag. There was no time for embarrassment - there were free things to collect! Using her arm, she snow plowed dozens of Covergirl's latest nail polish shades and Maybelline's newest lip stains into the bag, almost leaving the tables completely empty. Please note: we are still college students. We freak out when Chick-Fil-A gives away a free sandwich. An entire room of makeup was almost too much to handle. This was no time to be classy; this was every tuxedo-wearing brute for themselves.

When the bag was finally packed to the brim, CoCo took a deep breath of satisfaction. "Ah, thank you for the makeup… oh, and the prayer." With that they exchanged the 'I-don't-know-you too-well-but-I-feel-like-we-should-hug-so-I-will-lightly-pat your-back-and-keep-my-body-distant-from-yours' hug. CoCo went down to the locker room where I was trying to make the knot of my tie not look like such a discombobulated cluster. I could tell excitement was bursting out of every one of her powdered pores. Her makeover was beautiful, but it was the joy radiating from her soul that was the extra finishing touch. She told me about the free makeup, and opened up her bag and showed me what she got. She had twenty-three different shades of lip-gloss. TWENTY-THREE. This was complete cosmetic insanity. But before I even had time to be jealous, CoCo reminded me why we are such good friends. She shared with me. Our tuxedo pockets were stuffed that night like chipmunks cheeks, packed full of colorful tubes of gloss and compacts of powder. Every time we went back into the kitchen we would re-apply our new gloss. We felt pretty and feminine – despite our manly attire. Best shift ever. I love CoCo, and I love my glossy lips.

The Confection Resurrection

I had previously written about a $50,000 wedding cake that I wanted to punch in its third tier. But one thing I didn't realize is when you buy a cake at that price, it also comes with magical powers.

Another wedding, another bride, another shift. This one was held in our circular ballroom, one often used for wedding receptions. In the center of the ceiling hangs a chandelier the size of a fat manatee, and chubby naked babies are painted across the ceiling. I like to refer to this wedding as 'Malibu Barbie wedding,' even though we were in Palm Beach. The bride creepily resembled a perfectly proportionate Barbie doll, likely arriving for her special day in a pink cardboard box. She was gorgeous. Her decorating theme had a very tropical feel to it – dark pinks, lush orange and lime green covered everything. On either side of the door where guests entered sat six-foot-tall pineapples made completely out of hundreds of roses and fern leaves. They each weighed about 200 pounds, and it took a team of two men to hoist them onto their stands. I could only imagine how much those things cost. One giant pineapple was probably pricier than my entire flower budget at my wedding. On the day of my big event, we went to my friend's house and cut hydrangeas out of her mom's bushes to make my flower arrangements look slightly better than pathetic. I will never forget her sweet mother sitting in my kitchen surrounded by buckets and buckets of her home grown hydrangeas, tears forming in her eyes. She swore it was because she was just so happy for me, but the fact that all of her summer yard work was now lying in piles around her feet may have had something to do with it.

Back to the Malibu Barbie wedding. The tables were covered in alternating pink and burnt orange sequined tablecloths, which may sound tacky, but actually looked modern and crisp against the classic architecture of the ballroom. There were gigantic flower arrangements on every table, with four-foot-tall birds of paradise sticking out of their centers. Birds of paradise are an amazing flower, but they also look like they may come alive and slice your face off at any moment. The lighting was dim and candles lined the entire ballroom, sitting on the windowsills and casting a warm glow on the celebration.

The Barbie bride was blonde (of course), and probably a size two. Her dress was completely backless and made of lace, with a long train, very elegant and classic. One of my best friends from school, Kristin, was helping the bride in her suite before the ceremony. I met Kristin the first week of college at a beach campout. She has sun-bleached hair with hemp and seashells woven into it. She laughs louder than anyone I know, and has a sugar addiction like no other. I could not ask for a better creature to go through this young adult life with, wearing a tuxedo or not. Laughing with her as we sneak ice cream out of the back cooler or doing weird dances in our Grandma loafers behind our supervisors back always brightens a shift.

So while Kristin was helping the bride get ready, she complimented her on such a gorgeous gown. "It's vintage!" the bride chirped back. It *would* be a vintage gown – I suspect perfect Malibu Barbie brides would accept nothing less.

The ceremony came and went without a hitch, and people started pouring into the reception. The five-tier cake sat right in front of the entrance to the ballroom, the first thing guests' eyes were drawn to as they entered. It had its own table and a spotlight shining down upon it. Its white, sugary frosting sparkled in the light like freshly fallen snow. There were pink damask ribbons wrapped around the base of every tier, and a gigantic letter S covered completely in Swarovski crystals sat on the top, standing for the new couple's last name. It looked delicious, and I made a mental note to find a renegade piece to eat before the night was over.

The reception had an open bar, as there almost always is at the hotel.[14] People were flocking to it like crazed raccoons to a rancid Thanksgiving turkey carcass. Clearly they were going to be a heavy drinking group. The bar backs were running all over the place in a frenzied attempt to keep everything in stock.

A particularly loud woman had already gone back to the bar for three tequila sunrises, and the party had only been going an hour. Her hair was extra voluminous; it looked as if she may have been using one of those 'Bump-it' clips you can buy at Walgreens.[15] Her dress was floor length, bright purple and drenched in sequins, resembling the tablecloths, yet far more obnoxious. She stood out in the crowd like a mouse turd in a bowl of white rice. She had a very thick New York accent, and a laugh that resembled a garbage disposal trying to destroy a renegade spoon. She wore bright blue eye shadow swept back to her hairline, reminding me of pictures I had seen in the paper of Fantasy Fest held down in Key West every year. The woman was out of control.

The low-key arrival music faded out and the wedding band piled on stage to begin their night of keeping things funky. The first song on their list: "Poker Face" by Lady Gaga (long live the Lady!) Before they could even get through the "oh…oh oh oh oh oh…oh oh oh oh…" the purple glittery mess threw her arms up in the air and started recklessly shaking her hips. She started backing up and gesturing to someone standing near the back bar to follow her onto the dance floor. As she was shaking, backing up and gesturing, she forgot to look behind her at where she was going and her sequined booty ran right into the cake table, which collapsed upon impact.

---

[14] I couldn't afford an open bar at my wedding. At one point I think we considered buying a keg of beer, but somehow that idea never materialized. I am glad. I would forever remember my wedding as resembling a kegger, but with my Grandma present.

[15] Bump-its creep me out, but for some reason I still yearn to try one.

Emergency! Cake down! Cake down!

It buckled into a big, cakey, sugary mess and there was no possibility of recovery. Half of it was splattered across the carpet, half still remained on the toppled over table, and a little piece was stuck to the crazy lady's right butt cheek. Judging by the price of other cakes we have had at the hotel (cough-$50,000-cough), I was sure that one probably cost more than a couple hundred bucks. What a big, hot, waste of money.

The purple sparkle monster was too busy and boozy on the dance floor to even realize the destruction she just produced. The bride was now standing nearby, her eyes as wide as a bush baby's, her gaze drifting back and forth from the sugary mess, to the sequined mess on the dance floor. She didn't say a word, and her face became a darker shade of red with each second that passed. I thought I could see steam shooting out of her ears. I was terrified.

Almost instantly after the cake collapsed, a cluster of chefs, seeming even more frazzled and upset than the bride, hustled out and hoisted the pile of cake chaos off of the floor and onto a cart. With their tall white hats erect like little cake-making elves, they shuffled the sticky mound into the kitchen.

It was at that moment I witnessed a real live wedding cake miracle. A mere seven minutes later, the chefs wheeled the cart back out, and atop it sat the cake in perfect condition, looking better than it did pre-destruction. The party continued on like nothing ever happened. The purple glitter beast drank three more tequila sunrises, and the bride slow danced to Elton John with her father.

What a magical mystery. Someone call the *Boxcar Children*, because I want to get to the bottom of that confectionary miracle. But alas, since the *Boxcar Children* died with the 90's, I was forced to do my own investigative work into this case of the re-appearing sugared viand. After asking around a bit, a seasoned co-worker explained to me often extremely expensive cakes come with a "back up", in case of disasters such as this. That makes sense, but I have one issue. Where have all these "extra cakes" been hiding, and why have I not been able to consume them? However, the real question of the night was this: can the chefs take me back into their magical room and make me look better than when I went in? Not if I am still wearing this tuxedo. Sigh.

The Elderly Party Machine

I showed up at the hotel for my five o'clock shift at exactly 5:06, my typical amount of lateness. I wish every day I clocked in one exact minute before my shift began, not too early, and definitely not late. But the reality is, I don't think being perfectly on time is genetically programmed into my body. Usually before leaving for work, or any event I really don't want to attend, I find everything possible to do that prevents me getting out the door and getting on the road in a timely fashion. It will be the perfect time to leave, my shoes will be on, my purse slung over my shoulder, and my keys in my hand. Then, I will spot my coffee pot out of the corner of my eye and lustfully think "I must have a coffee right now, I must. Surely I can still be on time," when really I know that the four-minute brewing process will push me into the realm of lateness. But I brew anyway. Then, coffee in hand, I walk to the bathroom to have one last glance in the mirror before heading out and think "yikes, my ponytail is not at its perky best today." I will dink around trying to fix it for another three minutes. Then, I will look at my toothbrush and think "yes, another quick brush could do me good, especially now that I have this coffee to deal with." I spend the next seventy-five seconds thoroughly cleansing my chompers.

So, there you have it. It takes either a miracle or prescription for Adderall for me to be on time. I wish it was different, and I was 'that girl' who is always three minutes early, her frizz-free hair blowing lightly in the wind, her makeup perfect and her outfit professionally ironed. But with a brain as distracted as mine, I often get off track and wander around like a ninety-eight year old man who broke out of his nursing home to try and find a liquor store. Look, I am even off track right now, and have completely strayed from the story I originally set out to write. Back to business.

It was 5:06 and I was all clocked in. I checked the assignment board and saw I would be working in our largest ballroom for the evening. It is not as elegant as the others. Gaudy hotel carpet covers floor, and tracks line the ceiling where walls can be added to divide the space up into several smaller conference rooms if needed. It is built for function over beauty, and can hold up to 2,000 people. I walked upstairs and into the kitchen, where Craig was standing holding the paper run-down for the evening.

"Glad you could make it," he said to me, his face placid.

"I'm only eight minutes late, which qualifies as fashionable," I said, as I grabbed the paper from him and began scanning it for vital information.

"Be on time!" he snapped, and then got back to his speech. "This is a very high profile birthday party tonight. It is a VIP event, and an expensive one, too. The contact ordered way too many hors d'oeuvres so make sure you pass, pass, pass!"

I stopped listening to him once he said the word hors d'oeuvres, and began daydreaming about what delicious morsels I may be able to sneak throughout the night. I assured Craig of my superstar server skills, and headed to the ballroom to begin setting up my tables. When I stepped through the heavy wooden double doors, I saw he was not exaggerating, and this obviously was a very high profile and pricey event.

The usually ho-hum room was completely transformed. The décor was crisp and modern, with red lights casting a sultry burn over the room. There were dozens of cocktail tables set up near the back, and mini-living rooms arranged in the corners. Sleek white couches, mirrored end tables, and large, loudly patterned throw pillows were scattered about, giving me the strong desire to lie down and take a nap. I could see in the front right corner a platform and spotlight being set up behind large, gorgeous hanging white linens. I had seen a setup like this before – it meant some curvy young beauty would be dancing the night away behind the linen, with the shadow of her perfect silhouette viable for all the guests – adding to the sensuality of the décor.

In the front of the room was a huge stage. The band was already warming up, their vocals filling the large space and trickling down the hallways. The birthday boy must have been a complete hot shot to have such an extravagant party. I would guess it was probably some young Palm Beach real estate prodigy who split his time between the island, Manhattan and Paris. At least that was what I would do if I had enough money to throw a fiesta like that one.

Us servers began our usual hustle and bustle of setting the silverware, polishing the glasses and lighting the dozens of candles that were scattered throughout the room. An hour or so later the guests began to arrive. I had a perfect plate of coconut chicken with orange marmalade to pass, the deliciously greasy scent wafting up into my nose, making me suddenly aware of my ever-growing hunger pangs. I quickly tried to get rid of all of the chicken except for one, so I could meander back into the kitchen and eat it. The crowd was an interesting mix of people. Middle-aged socialites with large coifs, young overly-botoxed beauties and men young and old dressed in designer suits and shiny leather shoes. Drinks could not be served fast enough, and I got the sense that this crowd was going to be a little on the rowdy side.

I finally passed out all my chicken except a lone, perfect and delicious looking piece. I headed back into the kitchen to slyly consume my strategically lonely poultry chunk. Just as I was about to exit the ballroom, a fat man with a shiny bald head and bright pink tie stepped in front of me and put up his hand as if to say "halt." I did just that, and he reached to take the last coconut chicken off of my plate, dunking it so deep into the orange marmalade his fingertips came up covered in the sweet goo. I inwardly scowled at the overfed beast, as he just ate my only option for quieting my grumbling stomach. He took a cocktail napkin from me, wiped his fingers, tossed his crumpled trash onto my plate, and walked away without saying one word to me. Sigh. Was I nothing more than just a chicken-serving, tuxedo-wearing robot? Apparently.

I entered into the kitchen to get more food to pass, and saw Craig having a heated discussion with my co-worker, Frank. Frank is in his sixties, and is the kind of guy who you are never quite sure if he is cracking a joke or just going senile. I have come to the conclusion it is a combination of both. For example, Frank's favorite thing to do is assign a number to you for no apparent reason. We were standing near each other one night waiting for the guests to arrive, and Frank looked at me and said, "88858. That is your number, 88858."

"What? What are you talking about?"

"I gave you a lot of eight's," he said, "because eight's are like snowmen, and I like snowmen. I like you." Then he turned and walked away. That was the strangest, yet most interesting compliment I have ever received.

"Katie, Frank forgot to pull the salt and peppers from the basement, now there are none on the tables," Craig yelled over at me. "Go help him get some and get them out there right away."

Frank and I headed down the stairwell into the basement, just as the band switched over from their low key welcoming music to the bass-thumping, booty shaking "let's dance the night away" set. We arrived at the storeroom only to feel like we were stepping into some dank back room at a nightclub. The band was blaring out Usher's latest hit so loud above us the shelves were vibrating. In all my countless shifts, I have never heard a party get so loud that the music travels through the floor into the basement, let alone cause sturdy shelving to shiver like they caught a bad fever on the Oregon Trail. Frank and I quickly loaded the salt and pepper shakers onto a cart and trudged back upstairs. Frank was now covering his ears to block out the blaring Pitbull re-mix that only got louder and louder as we re-approached the ballroom. He shouted to me, "Whoever this hot shot is, he is going to be deaf by the time he is forty. You young kids always play your music too loud!"

"Whatever, Frank! Let's just get this over with," I yelled back, and we each grabbed as many salt and peppers as our glove covered hands would hold, and headed inside to start placing them on tables. Before I could place one shaker down, the lights in the entire ballroom went black and the crowd let out a startled cry. A low, deafening bass note blared from the speaker, and a voice filled the room as if it were God himself speaking.

"Ladies and gentlemen, he is the reason you are here, he is paying for your drinks, he is the man of the hour," the voice boomed out. Fake smoke filled the stage and white spotlights were darting about, building the anticipation. Who was this guy?

"Put your hands together," the voice continued, "foooooor the birthdayyy boyyyy." The band started playing a rap version of Happy Birthday, and I saw Frank again cover his ears and scowl. Sparks shot up from the stage, and bright spotlights flooded it. Through the fog I could see the outline of a person walking towards the front of the stage, very slowly. There appeared to be a large-breasted woman wearing a skimpy red mini-dress on one of his arms, his other was raised in the air waving to the crowd, which was now cheering as if this man were a rock star. As the fog cleared, more details became apparent. The hot shot birthday boy was anything but a young thirty-something having the time of his life. Instead of a tan, handsome, muscular young chap in a tailored suit, he was an eighty-five year old, writhed shell of a man. He was wearing a bright purple cigar jacket, black velvet slippers embroidered in gold thread, and oversized Ray-Ban sunglasses. He had a Quasimodo hump, which reminded me I should start taking calcium pills. As I watched him shuffle about the stage, I almost dropped my salt and pepper shakers when I saw him turn to his arm candy (who was probably in her mid twenties), and give her the sloppiest, wettest, longest kiss I ever have witnessed. Gag. I looked over at Frank, who was slowly shaking his head back and forth, hands still plastered over his ears, eyes wide with the same disbelief that I was feeling. The birthday boy was not a boy at all, but a grandpa. Perhaps even a great grandpa. This was almost too much for me to handle.

After his mid-stage make out session ended, he and his arm candy carefully left and went straight for the bar. The band started back up with their loud and funky beats and the guests stormed the dance floor. The spotlight behind the hanging linen in the front right corner flashed on, and the perfect, busty silhouette of a woman became visible. She swiveled her perfect hips, she dropped it like it was hot, and she whipped her waist-length hair back and forth, Willow Smith style. That anonymous woman had more curves than the California Coastal Highway, and her dance moves were borderline stripper. I thought it was creepy, but the crowd seemed to be into it.

The rest of the night, the birthday dinosaur was not seen without a Red Bull vodka in his hand. He made the rounds, greeting guests by giving glamorous double kisses to the cheeks of old friends and new acquaintances alike. He tore up the dance floor in the best way a man with such a crotchety back could, which was mostly a few feet shuffles and a snap every once in a while. His young beauty never left his side.

2:00 in the freaking morning rolled along, and the party was still going strong. There was no more food to be passed, and the servers were just being held captive so they could perform clean up duty when the birthday grandpa finally decided to call it a night. Out of boredom, I began walking around the room, apathetically picking up glasses and crumpled cocktail napkins smeared with lipstick and crumbs. As I neared the front corner of the room my curiosity was struck as to what that mystery dancing woman actually looked like, who, for the record, was still going strong despite the late hour. Was she as attractive as her silhouette suggested? I had to find out. And I mean, she wasn't actually nude behind that sheet, was she? I guess it wouldn't surprise me, as naked people tend to show up often at the hotel for some strange reason. I must see what this pop-it and lock-it woman looks like, I must.

So, I discretely continued with my glassware and trash pickup ploy, making sure my path was heading straight for the mystery women. Luckily, there was a small cocktail table piled with dirty glasses right next to the hanging linen shielding us from the dancer's true identity – a perfect alibi for my sneak peak session. I glanced around and saw nobody was paying attention to me, as they were too immersed in shaking their booties to the Lady Gaga song currently blasting from the speakers. I set my tray down and just went for it. I put my head behind the curtain, and there she was. Her back was to me and I see she was in fact not nude, thank goodness, but wearing a faded blue one-piece swimsuit. Her long hair was too perfectly blonde and shiny to be real, and I decided to myself she was either wearing a wig or had hair extensions. Just then, she whipped around to face me, too engrossed in her dance moves to notice my little eyes peering at her. When I get the frontal view, I quietly gasped in shock. The woman, who I had assumed to be a young twenty-something, was in fact old enough to have a twenty-year-old child. She had to be mid-fifties at least, her face covered in wrinkles and a few hair ridden moles sprouting on her cheek. Not only that, her faded blue swimsuit had a massive rip in it on her stomach, revealing a quarter-sized portion of her soft flesh. Couldn't she afford a new leotard? I guess dancing behind a sheet doesn't pay that well. Feeling the same shock that Dorothy did when she looked behind the curtain to reveal the true identity of the Wizard of Oz, I quickly grabbed my tray and hurried back to the kitchen, my mind trying to wrap around the bizarre party happening around me.

The festivities continued until about four in the morning, the birthday man and his aged silhouette dancer alive and kicking for every moment of it. With every rap song played and vodka the wrinkled party boy knocked back, I became more amazed at his liveliness. And with every booty shake and shimmy, I became more impressed at the energy of that ripened dancer. I can only hope I remember my own name at my eighty-fifth birthday party, let alone get down and dirty till the wee hours of the morning. And if I have dance moves like that woman when I am past forty, I will consider my life a success. These people put true meaning to the saying "age is just a number," even if that number is nearing triple digits.

The Bra: A Wedding Necessity

Another shift, another wedding – man, people get married a lot. This wedding stood out as slightly more glamorous than most. It appeared no detail was forgotten in the planning process, as each little morsel of the décor overflowed with style, elegance and beauty. The silver Swarovski crystal-encrusted tablecloths matched the rose napkins, which matched the pale pink toned lighting, which matched the signature pink champagne infused cocktails passed to guests as they arrived. All the plates and silverware were polished and sparkling under dozens of white Chinese lanterns that were hung from the ceiling. It was gorgeous, as weddings always seem to be at the hotel.

The ceremony took place in the one of the smaller ballrooms. Filled with about 200 people and just as many candles, the gold leaf ceiling glistened in the soft light. There was a traditional Jewish chuppah made entirely out of white roses and long windy twigs that towered over the whole room, filling it with a sweet scent. There were also lots of cute little men wearing yarmulkes roaming the halls, and a rabbi with a massive beard, so I knew that night would be yet another celebration of Jewish bliss. There was a string quartet playing, and a perfectly handsome groom standing up front awaiting his beautiful bride.

Again, it *appeared* no detail was left out of this joyous event. Well, except for one small detail that hands down will be the *most* remembered part of the entire matrimonial celebration.

Before the ceremony, I was assigned to stand near the entrance to pass out programs and yarmulkes. This had been a fairly uneventful task, until a man, who introduced himself to me as Great Uncle Billy, leaned in close to my ear and yelled, "Do you like cats?" before shuffling away to his seat.

Soon after that, the music picked up and the bridal party slowly began trickling into the room. I quickly stepped to the side and discreetly planted myself near the back of the room, as I am a woman and enjoy watching wedding ceremonies for some unknown stupid reason that is programed into my genes.[16] After the grandmothers, with their teased hair and tacky, over-adorned dress suits were escorted down the aisle, the bridesmaids began to enter. From the back of the room I could tell they all had glowing tanned skin and gorgeous champagne colored floor-length gowns. Their hair was elegantly swept away from their faces, and they all wore matching diamond bracelets. As they slowly began to trickle down the aisle, I noticed a few peculiar facial expressions from some of the guests. Then, in between verses of Pachelbel's Cannon, I could hear quiet gasps and low, gossipy mummers. Something funky was going on. Lucky for me, I watch a lot of CSI and have trained myself to be freakishly observant. I followed the gaze of the seemingly appalled guests, and all of their eyes appeared to be falling upon the chest region of each bridesmaid. It instantly became apparent what had captured their attention. The one, tiny detail that this bride-of-wonders had forgotten, was to tell her bridesmaids to wear a bra. All five of them were channeling their inner hippy and letting their lady pillows roam free beneath their thin couture gowns. I am not sure if you have been in a South Florida hotel recently, but usually the air conditioning is cranked to such a frigid level the Abominable Snowman could likely live comfortably. All of the bridesmaids' nipples were awake and alert, capturing the attention of every man and woman present. Poor Great Uncle Billy in the third row had to take a puff of his inhaler to prevent himself from entering into cardiac arrest at the sight of such a

---

[16] This is the same stupid feminine attribute that causes me to ugly cry over a sentimental toilet paper commercial, or stare longingly at a baby like it was a double chocolate cheesecake.

feminine body part overload. He probably hadn't seen that many nipples since his goat milking days back in the 1960's.[17]

Finally, all five bridesmaids and all ten of their nips had made their descent down the aisle, and were perfectly lined up at the front of the room like a clan of overly dressed cabaret dancers. They were all beaming, (in more ways than one), as the bride began walking down the aisle. Thank goodness she remembered to make a trip to Victoria Secret before her big day. Ten nips were more than enough for Great Uncle Billy to handle at once – twelve could have pushed him over the edge.

The bride arrived under the chuppah and the rabbi began the ceremony. It wasn't long into it when her almost-husband switched from groom mode back to plain old man mode. His eyes began drifting away from those of his beloved bride, over her shoulder to where the clan of bra-less babes were standing. He too had now noticed their nipple extravaganza and had fallen victim to their evil powers.

After he glanced four or five times in the direction of the boobs, the bride became curious as to what was distracting him. She followed his gaze and quickly realized what he had been staring at. Her pink painted mouth gaped open in disgust at her mans wayward glances. She whipped her head back around, gave her groom a death stare and a small punch on his arm. The crowd tried to stifle their laughter with little success, except for Great Uncle Billy, who had now fallen asleep and was slightly drooling. The bride, however, did not find the grooms behavior very amusing. She pouted through her entire vows.

Finally, the ceremony wrapped up and the girls and their headlights led the way into the reception. I walked around the corner towards the kitchen to grab a couple bottles of champagne, and saw the bride laying into her now husband about his wandering eyes. His repeated attempts at apologies were not helping. Oh weddings, so romantic.

The main course that night was delicious, (trust me I know, I "sampled" one), and the music was soul shaking.

---

[17] Goats have nipples, right?

Expensive champagne was sipped on and tiny little beautifully sculpted desserts were passed around on silver trays. But even with all that money spent on gorgeous food, drinks and decorations, one thing will remain in the memories of all 200 guests in attendance: boobs.

Porky Judaism

When I arrived at work for this particular event, I noticed an ambulance pulled up onto the property by the entrance to our largest ballroom. I immediately grew concerned that the random, wildly rich old woman who lived on the entire top floor of the hotel had kicked the bucket, and I became sad for her, and her now orphaned cat. But when I got closer to the ambulance I realized there was a giant star of David on it and writing in Hebrew. Hmm… the context clues now suggested that a rabbi has fallen ill and requested kosher health care. However, I soon learned from a passing coworker that there was not an injured rabbi, and the ambulance was nothing more than an extremely unusual party decoration. The event was going to be a fundraiser to help purchase ambulances in Israel, which is great – I just question their party decorating skills.

During the pre-party meeting, Craig explained to us the charity has held this fundraiser at the hotel for the past five years, and just about every Jewish person in South Florida attends. Please note – this event is nothing new for the hotel, which makes the proceeding events even more ridiculous.

Set up came and went with all the excitement of a standardized math test. My faded black tube socks were starting to sag and I already had a stain on my white gloves, so I knew it was about time to serve.

I went back into the kitchen to pick up the hors d'oeuvres I had been assigned to pass. The chef handed me a tray piled with of asparagus smeared in garlicky cheese and wrapped in prosciutto. Prosciutto, just to clarify, is pork. And by that I mean cold, slimy, thinly sliced, questionably raw looking pork.

Breaking news people – most Jewish people don't eat pork. They basically never have. This is nothing new. Yet someone, somewhere thought it was a great idea to throw it on the menu. I looked at the pork wrapped around the green stems and I wondered, should I say something? I didn't think this crowd was going to be a big fan of the practically still squealing snacks. I found Craig, who was in the back of the kitchen organizing packets of Splenda so the labels all faced the same direction.

"Craig, this is pork. If I go out there with this, someone may judo chop their yarmulke at my gullet."

He didn't even look up from his artificial sweeteners. "Just serve them. The party planner ordered them, and will get mad if we don't."

"Well, Craig, who exactly was that so-called party planner? Did you give them a background check, because if I had to guess, it probably was an undercover Palestine trying to sabotage the Israelites snacking pleasures. This is pork, Craig. Jewish people don't eat pork."

Hors d'oeuvres can get quite political if you're not careful.

"You are pork!" Craig snapped at me. "Now just go serve those!"

Did he just call me fat? I shrugged it off and did what I was told. I ventured out into the sea of guests with slimy pork in hand. I put on my best 'I-am-at-work-and-supposed-to-be-smiling' smile and did my thing. I offered one person a porky treat. I got a funny look and a "no thanks." Okay – that went well, I thought. Perhaps they just were not hungry, or they were on the socialite starvation diet. I offered it to a woman nearby, and I got a "What is that?"

"Prosciutto…which *is* pork." I just wanted to cover my bases. She responded with the classic 'turn my head, put my nose in the air, because I am so rich and don't speak to people in tuxedos unless they look like George Clooney,' which is Palm Beach code for "no thank you." You are so welcome for my service, wealthy America.

A man with a large midsection and bad hairpiece saw my plate of goods, and stopped me to inquire about what I was passing. "Pork!" I tensed my face in case he slapped me. But he did just the opposite. He threw sneaky sideway glances around to see if there was a Rabbi lingering in sight. The coast was clear. He stuffed a couple into his mouth and a few more into his coat pockets for later. He gave me a wink, put his finger to his lips and mouthed a silent 'shhh.' Weird. So weird.

I spotted my friend Sam in the corner of the room working at the bar. I was walking towards her to fill her in on my pork issue and chat about how annoying Craig was, when I passed a man talking very loudly and obnoxiously. His long beard shook with every word and he was completely immersed in his colorful conversation. He gave a half glance at the food, grabbed one and shoved it into his bearded mouth before I could even explain to him what it was. His eyes got wide. His side curls started quivering with anger. *"Is… this… PORK?"*

"Ah… yes. It is." And those were the magic words that made crap hit the fan. The man flipped out – and me, the poor pork holding necktie wearing waitress got the brunt of his anger. "I don't know who you think you are, or what you think you are doing, but we are all JEWISH here if you haven't noticed! And that means, little girl, that we DON'T EAT PORK."

I half wanted to point to the guy who just ate five servings of it, but decided it would not be a good time to throw him under the bus. Despite my apologies and feeble head nods in agreement with him, the man did not calm down. He flailed his arms, demanded to speak to a manager, and basically made me feel worse than the dead pig he ate just for trying to do my job.

I grudgingly endured about thirty-two more seconds of his yelling before I peaced-out and went to find Craig, who was still in the kitchen, now filling up dozens of baskets with bread.

"Craig! A guy almost punched me in the face for feeding him pork. I think he was yelling in Hebrew at one point, which has to be serious."

"Throw it all in the trash," he said placidly, before returning to his breadbasket adventuring.

So, as we should have done in the first place, I began the task of dumping the untouched food into the trash. I probably threw away one hundred of the prosciutto hors d'oeuvres. And please note, for no other reason besides the fact that we work on Palm Beach Island, the hors d'oeuvres are priced at five dollars a pop. I threw away hundreds of dollars of asparagus and weird bacon. Goodbye, overly priced treat, goodbye.

But I must be honest. I am not Jewish. And I love prosciutto. And asparagus. And especially Boursin cheese. When mixed together it is the best crunchy, cheesy, salty mess you have ever tasted. Before I tossed them all away, I tossed a couple in my belly. I thank you, ancient Jewish traditions, for on that night, you kept me fed.

Condoleezza Rice Pudding

I arrived at work one evening dragging my feet as I entered the hotel's dungeon basement and wearily swiped my card to sign in, making sure I sighed loudly enough while doing so that anyone in a three foot radius could hear my despair. Here we go again, another ride on the waitressing train. Hoot Hoot. I walked upstairs, opened the door to the ballroom and was once again transported to a world that doesn't know what it's like to have to wear non-slip loafers to work, or learn to tie a tie as an eighteen year old female. I stepped into a world that only knew glamour, wealth, and luxury. Maybe if I didn't look down at how I was dressed, I could pretend to be a part of the glam life instead of just the servant wearing a used tuxedo with ripped pocket lining.

I found Craig and was handed the paper that explained what we would be doing for the evening. I looked to see who my serving partner would be, but couldn't find my name.

"Craig, why am I not on the sheet?" I asked, hoping the answer would be I had been assigned to taste test every ice cream sundae in the back cooler before they were to be served.

"You're not with us, they moved you to another party," he said over his left shoulder as he power walked out of the ballroom, likely to take on some other random piece of hotel business.

Crap. I looked at Kyle, Kristin and CoCo, knowing that was probably the last time I would see them that night. Parting with them almost made me want to cry a few tears on my polyester sleeve. Don't pull me from this room of glamour, beauty, and friendship! Let me stay, Craig, let me stay.

But such was my waitressing fate for that evening. Instead of making work semi-bearable by working side by side with friends in a gorgeous party, I was assigned to a tiny ballroom with retractable walls and ugly carpet. I learned it was going to be a party of thirty, and the only other person working was creepy old Amos, the elderly man who only opened his mouth to yell at me for menial tasks like folding the napkins a few degrees off from the correct angle. During my time at the hotel, there had only been one time in recorded history I saw Amos smile. He had stolen a roll, and was outside ripping it to shreds and feeding it to pigeons. For some reason, feeding these birds made him intensely happy ... a little too happy. He threw his head back and laughed like a psychopath with every new pigeon that came along. It was a terrifying scene to witness. With that image in my mind, I knew I had a long night ahead of me.

I walked back into the kitchen to go round up some silverware when I spotted three men with short haircuts, shady eyes and an American flag pin on their lapels. If I looked close enough, I could see clear curled wires running from behind their ears into their jackets. Yes – the secret service! I always get excited when these guys roll around for two reasons: one, it makes me feel like I am part of one of those cheesy cop shows I devour as if they were classic literature. Two, it means we have a big-shot in our midst, which always makes the night more exciting.

Now, being a secret service man sounds really exciting, but let's break it down for a second. For the majority of the night, all these guys were allowed to do was stand in one place and stare at paint peeling off the walls, as the person they were protecting was inside the party having a grand old time. Boring. I could tell they were yearning for some excitement, so I walked my little self over there and began slyly probing as to who they were working for. Some may call it flirting, but I prefer investigative journalism.

As I expected they were very willing to chat, and they quickly gave me the scoop - Condoleezza Rice was in our hotel.

For many of you reading this, the words Condoleezza Rice may spark no feelings inside of you except boredom, confusion, or perhaps make you crave Chinese food. But I, the young inspiring journalist with a slight CNN addiction, was star struck. I quickly daydreamed about our pending encounter:

"Oh Condo, may I call you Condo? Allow me to get you a nice strong drink, perhaps five. Then we can relax, chat, and I will keep getting you drinks until you spill every secret of the Bush presidency and give me all the details on the latest happenings at Area 51. Let's be best friends."

After I finished with my pathetic daydream, I asked the men where she was at this very moment in time. The beefiest one on the right looked over his shoulders, shifted his eyes left and right, then pressed his magical American flag pin and quietly said into it, "Blue 52, when will the eagle land?" Oh my gosh. Real, live secret service code. I was completely enamored.

"She will be coming down the elevator in about five minutes. If you wait here, you can meet her," the man said, while the thick necked guy on his left cracked his knuckles and sniffed loudly.

Well, well, well... it looked like my lame-o night had taken a turn for the better. So I stood there with the three guys, all of us wearing black suits but me being the only one with womanly curves underneath - at least I sure hoped I was the only one. I continued to make small chat with the guys, and kept my hands clasped behind my back to make it look like I was supposed to be standing there. Faking looking busy is practically the first lesson you learn as a waitress. Standing with authority is only second to walking briskly as if you had something extremely important to do, when in reality you are probably just headed to the cooler to steal a soda.

After a few more minutes of chit chat, the elevator numbers beeped and began to descend: fifth floor, fourth floor, third floor... she was almost in our midst when CODE RED! Craig rounded the corner, spotted me, gasped and charged toward me like we were about to participate in the Ultimate Fighting Championship.

"Katie, get out of here! Go back to your party!" he barked as he grabbed my shoulders and shoved me towards the kitchen. As he hustled me I tried to explain my Condoleezza situation, but he wouldn't have it. He gave me an evil look as he shut the kitchen door behind me. Humph. I crossed my arms in frustration.

I sat there for a second, not wanting to get back to actually working. I decided to peek my head out of the door, to see if I could still catch a glimpse of Condo Rice, and there she was, standing amidst her secret service men, and with a flustered assistant standing at her side. Condo's hair was blown out to make a perfect bubble around her freshly made up face. She had on a one-shoulder gown that fell straight to the floor. It was timeless yet in style at the same time. Who knew the former secretary of state would be dressed so fashionably? I imagined her to have on an unflattering colored pant suit like some *other* secretary of state we all know who shall remain nameless. Coughhillaryclintoncough.

But then, I noticed someone else standing in the gaggle of spectators: Craig. He was right there, front and center for the Condoleezza Rice meet and greet. I watched him as he plastered his best "five star service" smile on his face, shook her hand and showered her with flattery and small talk. That son-of-a-B. He had the audacity to shove me in the back kitchen as if I were some sort of deformed servant troll that was not to be seen wandering the halls of the hotel, just so he could take my spot in the excitement.

As I watched this scene play out from behind the kitchen door my frustration grew, and I became all the more motivated to graduate college and begin my journalism career. I yearned to be the one wearing glamorous gowns and mingling with the beautiful and powerful leaders of our nation. I yearned for the day I could come back to this hotel and eat a filet mignon at a table with silverware, not with dirty hands behind closed doors. I wanted to one day come back here and shove Craig into the back kitchen like a hotel troll, while I grabbed a glass of champagne and let out small fake laughs in true socialite fashion.

After three more seconds of watching Craig and his pathetic swooning, I decided to take action. I busted open the swinging kitchen door and glared at the back of Craig's head so hard I thought lasers would shoot out his eyes. Then I adjusted my tuxedo jacket, smoothed the frizz on my ponytail, and walked over to where the action was. As I strolled over towards them, I held my chin high with semi-fake confidence. While I was silently rehearsing what I would say to Condo when I introduced myself, I didn't notice the corner of a rug was overturned, and I tripped. Hard. I fell on all fours, and Condo, the secret service men and good 'ole Craig saw the whole thing happen.

"Ah… I'm okay!" I called out, my face turning the same deep shade of red as the piece of carpet that just took me down. They all stared at me blankly as I picked myself up off the ground. Silence blanketed the hallway like an itchy wool sweater. I quickly tuned and headed back into the kitchen just as the secret service men began escorting Condoleezza down the hall towards her party. Just when I thought I found solitude to shake off my embarrassment, Craig busted through the swinging doors, shoved a silver tray into my hands, and pointed towards the ballroom I was supposed to be working in. He said nothing – just stared at me with a look of pure disdain. I slowly turned and walked toward the rest of my night of servanthood, this time making sure to look where I was stepping.

Coffee on Silk: The Hottest Accessory

If you ever have been a server, you have had a moment like this. You know, when you clumsily slip, trip, and spill the darkest possible liquid on the lightest possible piece of clothing in a five-foot radius. No, you couldn't have spilled the glass of sprite or ice water onto your customer, it only makes sense that you spill the neon blue margarita. And no, it couldn't have landed on the nice gothic person wearing all black, it has to land on the snobby woman wearing brand new white pants, and a white tank top. Such is the way of life.

This was one of those terrible server moments when I wished I had decided to work in retail instead of the food industry. Side note - to all of the ladies wearing white outfits when going out to a restaurant or a fancy-schmancy banquet, please stop it. We will find you, and we will spill on you. It is just waiter fate.

It was a really long week. I had been working my butt off at my job and at school. I was extremely tired, and extremely out of it. It was really humid out so my hair was being unruly and frizzy, and I had lost my credit card the night before and I had no clue where. I was a big hot mess. The time of the night approached to go around and ask everyone at my table if they would like coffee, only to have them accept, not drink it and then I have to clean up dozens of cups of cold java. Joyous.

We serve the coffee in these silver pots that look like they are heirlooms belonging to the Queen of England. They feel like they weigh ten pounds each, and that's when they are empty. They are not the most sensible coffee serving contraptions, but they meet the hotels standards of fanciness, so that is what we used. I was worrying about my lost credit card and trying to reassure myself that it would all work out, and was completely distracted. For some reason, I thought it would be a good idea to hold the decaf and the regular pots at the same time, one in each hand, as I went around to serve the extremely hot beverage. The double coffee pot hold goes against all written and unwritten waiter rules, as it is likely to end in one big caffeinated disaster. But in my current distracted state, I just didn't notice.

I trudged to my first table, pots in hand filled to the brim with piping hot coffee. A little splashed out of the silver spouts with every step. The first woman I decided to serve, of course, was wearing a white, silk, floor-length gown. It had delicate straps and scooped really low down her tanned back, revealing her knobby spine.

You know when guys awkwardly stare at hot girls? Well, I do that about articles of clothing. If a woman is wearing something I adore, I stare at it with no shame. Her dress was gorgeous, and I was staring at it like a thirteen-year-old boy would stare at his buxom algebra teacher. I offered her coffee.

"Regular," she replied, without looking at me.

I tipped the pot of regular, carefully making sure it poured directly into her little cup. As far as I could see, I was successful. The coffee landed right in her mug perfectly, and I silently congratulated myself on being such a superstar server.

But alas! Not so fast, oh silent congratulator. In my distracted state, I tipped the other pot of coffee in sequence, and the steamy, dark coffee spilled down her back and all over her gown.

"Yeaaaahhheheeeeeeeaaaoooooooooooooottttt!" she screamed. After much contemplation, I have decided this is the best possible way to spell out the demon noise she emulated. Try to sound it out – unless you are in public or lying next to a peacefully sleeping spouse.

The woman slowly turned around to face me, her shoulders shuddering and her fists clenched. Her face was as red as the beet salad I served her earlier that evening, and her sculpted eyebrows were scrunched so close together in rage that they looked like a Frida Kahlo uni-brow. And, if I remember correctly, her hair turned into a cluster of snakes like Medusa, and her eyes began glowing neon green.[18]

Fighting through her rage, she managed to stammer, "THIS... IS... GUCCI!!!"

Gucci. Awesome. Why couldn't I have worked at a place where guests thought designer clothes came from the Isaac Mizrahi collection at Target, not ten thousand dollar gowns? I was so screwed.

"Oh...oh my," I stammered. I desperately tried to do something to help, but my arms were handicapped by the obnoxiously weighty coffee pots. Five people from her table were pathetically blotting her with napkins, and I was just standing there like a loser, attempting to apologize.

"I am so, so sorry. Oh my gosh, so sorry," I rambled on, and she seemingly became more angry with every word I uttered.

"Arghhhhh!" she cried out, and pushed all blotters off of her. She turned and marched straight over to Craig, who had quickly entered the room when he heard the woman's birthing wildebeest cries echoing in the massive ballroom. Every angered click of her stilettos across the hard ballroom floor seemed to stab me right in the eye. I felt like the ultimate douche. She started screaming at Craig, pointing with her manicured nails in my direction. Bits of spit caught the light and glistened in the air as they burst out of her mouth and fell onto Craig's face like a light rain shower. Fifteen minutes went by and she was still yelling at him. An *hour* passed and she was still with him, although by this time he had somehow managed to calm her down enough to make her Medusa snake hair disappear.

---

[18] Yes, she transformed into a mythological creature...deal with it. Most rich people have magical powers we are not aware of. I mean, how do you think they get their money to begin with? Money spells, duh.

Well, farewell, college job. It was nice while it lasted, kind of. Clearly Craig was about to walk over to me and tell me in his best Indian version of Donald Trump, "You're fired." Either that, or he was going to slap me across the face.

The woman finally left and headed toward the elevator, most likely going upstairs to her room to change. Craig was still standing in the same place, looking as if he was thinking hard about something, which at this point I could only assume was his plot to murder me. I walked over to him with great apprehension to face my demons.

"Craig, I am so, so, so sorry," I said, feeling like the kitchen sludge on the bottom of his shoe. I mean, I just scorched a woman's back with coffee and ruined a gown that probably cost more than a semester of tuition. It didn't get much worse as a server. "I've just had a terrible week, I was distracted, I don't know what... "

He held up his slender hand to stop me, and uttered the most shocking words I have heard thus far at the hotel.

"Oh, it's okay, don't worry about it. Things like this happen." He shrugged and walked back into the kitchen.

I stood there. Blinked. Blinked again, cocked my head, shrugged my own shoulders, and walked back to my table. Where was the ream out session? Where was the physical abuse? Where was the pink slip and shove out the door? I mean, I may have just gave a lady first degree burns...why am I not in trouble? Then it hit me. The hotel has so much money that accidents like that don't really matter. We can buy that woman a new dress and pay for her skin graft, no problem. I realized money was no object at my place of employment, nor to the people I serve. She could probably buy twenty gowns to replace it if she wanted, although I was sure the hotel would foot her bill. This abundance of wealth is a concept foreign to my middle class Midwest upbringing. At that moment, I felt oddly liberated, and a little less uptight about my job, knowing that just about anything I do wrong can be fixed by the unbelievable amounts of money we have.

For example, sometimes we pass food on $200 Versace plates. They are red and have an intricate design all around their lip, with little Geisha women woven throughout and detailed with real gold. (I think they are ugly, but that is not the point.) Before, I was always terrified I was going to drop one and have to fork over two paychecks to foot the bill. Now, I am not scared at all. Heck, I could probably smash five and nobody would really care. Of course, I am still careful when using them, because breaking anything worth that much makes me sick to think about. But if I did, no problem! According to Craig, things like that happen. Money – the solver of all the world's problems, but at the same time a major cause. I mean, what kind of crazy person spends $200 on an ugly plate? That is the real issue here. If you are going to spend that much on something you eat off of, it should at least have a hologram of Justin Bieber on it or something. That, I would never break. Ever.

24k Gold Human

When people throw a party at the hotel, it is more common than not that they will hire some insanely impressive form of entertainment to woo their guests. Sometimes cages of live animals are shipped in and set up around the room like living, breathing decor. You can actually hold amazingly cute animals like my personal favorite, a baby Koala named Walter. Once, this seemingly innocent Walter creature took a duker right on a ladies designer gown as she was holding him. That part was for the server's entertainment, obviously.

But if it's not baby animals, it is something else amazing. Sometimes there will be a performance by slender, bendy contortionists that make the plate of linguini sitting in front of the guests suddenly seem unappetizing. Or an artist who stands on stage and in four minutes flat produces a massive mural of the planet earth with a big heart around it, and every one claps and oohs and ahhs over the cheesy painting. My point being, the entertainment is always different. When I show up at work for the night, I never really know what to expect.

When I walked into the ballroom on this particular day, I found out the function was yet another charity event, which to me is always an interesting term when used at the hotel. When I think of a charity, I think of painting a house for an old knotted woman, or going to Mexico and fixing the roof on a school; anything dirty, sweaty and selfless. But in the case of Palm Beach, charity events usually come complete with an auction where one can bid on things like a week skiing in Vail, a tour of

Lilly Pulitzer's home and a luncheon with the great floral freak herself, or a pair of earrings that cost more than Prince William's underwear collection. It seems unreal to me, but some people are able to at a whim throw down $15,000 dollars for a week in a Hawaii beach home, flight not included. So weird.

But even though I find the lavish and spontaneous spending quite daunting, it really does go for a good cause, so we must give credit where credit is due. However, this version of charity still freaks me out. I am always tempted to grab the microphone from the auctioneer and offer up someone the opportunity to pay my student loans. I mean, if you can drop twenty grand on a designer luggage set, I think you can help a sister out. And finally, whenever they are raising money for some cause related to hunger, I get confused at where the whole concept of eating a $300 meal really plays into the scenario, but hey – no judgments. Okay maybe a little, but I am trying to fight it. It is all for a good cause.

Anyway, it was one of *those* charity events. No sweat or physical contact with the needy required, just lavish gowns, plumped glossed lips and a big checkbook. It was to be a silent auction night, so no need for the obnoxious announcer asking over and over for someone to bid on the prize nobody really seems interested in, like horse grooming lessons or a gift basket filled with random hair care products. Light laughter flitted through the air, and fingers weighed down by massive diamond rings lightly grabbed at the prosciutto and cantaloupe hors d'oeuvres, but passed on the fried goat cheese and artichoke hearts. (Which, for the record, are amazing. I salivate at the thought of them, but only slightly and not in an extremely off putting, spit everywhere kind of way – just so we are clear on my spit producing habits.)

Cocktail hour came and went. The guests had written their gigantic silent auction bids on the paper, and began to take their seats at the dinner tables. First course was served, a marinated grilled portabella mushroom with Mandarin oranges, scallions, cornbread croutons and sundried tomatoes, all topped with Valencia orange vinaigrette. Yum. As people began daintily picking at their salads, it was time for the entertainment to begin. What would it be that night? Japanese drummers? Sequin-wearing acrobats? N-Sync reincarnated from the musical grave?

No. I wish it were one of those things. I especially wished it had been N-Sync, 1999 style. But instead of a young, curly-haired Justin Timberlake with terrible, orange-blonde dyed hair, out walked a woman.

Not just any woman.

A naked woman.

Okay, I am slightly exaggerating; she was wearing a tiny thong. She did have her dignity!

The instant this naked chick walked out, every male server in the room just about poured wine in the guests' laps. While their minds had wandered to nude land, I was thinking to myself, why am I surprised? It's Palm Beach! Anything really goes if you slap a big 'ole price tag on it and call it art. So the thong woman stood in the center of the ballroom to begin her "performance." Perhaps she would tap dance? Sing? What could her nude talent possibly be?

A man walked out wearing a beret, and he had a terrible mustache that curled up at the edges. He was carrying a fancy-looking paint can and a huge paintbrush. He approached the nude and dipped the brush into the paint. When he pulled it out, we all saw that his paint can was filled with liquid gold, and he brushed a streak on the naked woman. Please note, this was not just gold paint, but actual *gold*. I verified this fact with Craig. What do you think this is, the Holiday Inn? The hotel is a class establishment – and we ONLY paint our naked folks with precious metals, obviously.

He proceeded to paint the woman gold, one inch at a time. Meanwhile, the serving standards of the male portion of the staff had dropped considerably, as they all seemed to be quite enthralled by the "artistic value" the entertainment had to offer. While I was hustling around my tables picking up my partners slack, I couldn't help but wonder how much that woman was getting paid to just stand there and be stared at like a hunk of steak in a tiger den. And what is a worse job – having to wear a tuxedo to work, or having to wear nothing at all? Seeing her stand there in all her fleshy glory actually made me thankful for my polyester death suit I was forced to wear night after night. I mean, at least it keeps me warm when the air conditioner gets turned up too high.

Eventually the woman's entire body was covered in the gold paint, including all of her most shameful areas. She began walking around the room like a living statue, smiling and posing at random spots. At one point, she stood a little too close to the chair of an elderly lady wearing a distinguished looking hat, and the lady shooed her away as if she were a gold colored pigeon. She just continued waltzing around with this creepy smile plastered across her face, causing her paint covered skin to crease at the corner of her eyes. As I watched her parade around the room, the light reflecting off her metallic flesh, I began to wonder something: could I take this woman into the jewelry store and trade her in for a wedding ring upgrade? Or could I mail her to one of those "cash for your gold" services and make a profit? I wonder what their going rate for one 14-karat human is? And most importantly, could I rent her out for private events? It was my Great Uncle Frank's birthday the next week – I was sure he would appreciate this woman's…talent? Actually – scratch that idea. I wouldn't want him to croak from a heart attack, as he is my favorite person to beat in Scrabble.

Polygamy? Perhaps.

I'm going to share with you one of the most beautiful wedding ceremonies I have ever seen. The small ballroom was packed so full of lavender roses and candles that the guests looked like they were sitting in a garden, minus the bees and scorching Florida sun. The floral scent was strong and sweet. I love the smell of roses. I know everyone does, but I do more than most. It reminds me of when I was just thirteen years old, and my best friend gave Kyle the combination to my locker on Valentine's Day. After I walked out of a particularly terrible algebra class, I opened it up to find it filled with the flowers, and a toy gorilla that sang "Wild Thing." When I pressed the gorilla's hand and he began to sing and dance, every girl within a fifteen foot radius of my locker looked over and saw what Kyle did for me and was instantly jealous, which, to a pathetic thirteen year old, is the best thing ever.

Back to the wedding. A cluster of roses anchored every row along the center aisle. A chuppah made out of willow branches intertwined with more lavender colored roses and white lilies was at the front of the room. A five-piece orchestra was shoved into the front corner of the room ready to entice the guests with their notes of musical genius. The room was literally packed with so much beauty it seemed to almost overflow into the hallway.

I had been working in the kitchen helping fill the baskets of bread for dinner, so I had yet to see the bride. Craig came in and asked me to go hold a tray of yarmulkes in front of the ceremony entrance. I went, but with inner reluctance, for being the yarmulke girl requires me to hold a huge and heavy antique silver tray piled high with the tiny hats, and plaster on a fake smile until all the guests are seated. When I am finally finished my arms are so numb and useless I feel like a store mannequin with loose shoulder sockets. The only thing entertaining about being the yarmulke girl is watching the guests deal with putting the yarmulke on their head. One would think this mundane task would be a non-issue, but it always becomes a dramatic task for at least a handful of guests.

There are a couple scenarios that happen without fail every time I am on yarmulke duty. The first is old, balding men asking me if I have a bobby pin to secure the hat to their head. I have been asked this several times, at several different weddings. Really? After the fourth hairless man asked me this question, I resisted the urge to say "Sir, do I look like a Walgreens to you? And let's be honest, you are bald. Where would you even attach the bobby pin? You would probably have better luck with double stick tape." But in the spirit of holy matrimony,(and the necessity for keeping my job)(and the fact I am way too passive to ever say such confrontational sass), I refrained from such words.

The other entertaining scenario is when non-Jewish guests approach my tray of yarmulkes. They look at the pile of little hats with a confused and uncomfortable facial expression that somewhat resembles that of an infant ailed with gastric discomfort. They glance around and hesitantly take one off the tray, not quite sure if they are invited to join in on the hat wearing fun. Then, since this is their first yarmulke experience, they are unsure of what exactly to do. They bumble around doing silly things like blotting their sweat with it and shoving it into their pocket, or putting it over their eye and making a pirate noise nobody laughs at. While this yarmulke confusion is likely uncomfortable for the guest, it serves as my only source of entertainment at the moment. I thoroughly enjoy watching them squirm about in their cloud of religious disarray.

Soon all the guests were seated, all the tiny hats were taken from my tray, and my arms were screaming at me to give them a break. The orchestra music picked up, signaling that the ceremony was about to begin. I heard muffled talking and footsteps around the corner, and I assumed it was the wedding party approaching, so I pressed myself against the hallway wall to try to blend in, as I wanted to see what kind of dress the bride was wearing.

The first person to round the corner was the hotel's large and terribly frightening wedding coordinator, Pam. Pam's job is to basically suck up to every bride willing to lay down the big bucks for a wedding at the hotel. She is a supervisor and could get us fired if we even sneezed wrong, so we are supposed to be on our best behavior whenever she is around. If she caught me eating food I would probably get canned. Ironically, she probably eats more than any other employee around. Every time I walk into the kitchen she is stuffing her little chubby cheeks with something delectable. She claims it is to make sure the food is acceptable to serve. I claim the chick just has a huge appetite.

Anyway, Pam was barreling down the hallway in her usual dramatic fashion, shushing everyone in her path, even if they were already silent. Once she finished with making sure everyone around her was as quiet as an introverted librarian, the wedding party rounded the corner. Yes! Front row seat to someone else's matrimonial bliss. I love watching wedding parties walk down the aisle. Sometimes, to my own embarrassment, I get really lame and mushy, and a single tear will roll down my cheek. I discreetly wipe it away with my white serving gloves, only to get a clump of garlic in my eye or some mystery sticky substance smeared across my cheek. I hate those gloves.

But when I saw this wedding party, I didn't tear up; rather, I almost choked on my gum. I understand that sometimes people feel the need to throw all of their sorority sisters into their wedding party, so they have ten or so bridesmaids. And of course there always is the smelly sister-in-law that you feel compelled to add in, or your fiancé's terribly odd second cousin you only met once who asks if she can be a bridesmaid and you don't have the heart to decline her request. Things like this happen, it's understandable. Sometimes, wedding parties get big.

But this wedding, well, it was really big. Bigger than Pam's appetite. As the party continued to round the corner, my eyes widened as I took count. The bride had twenty-five bridesmaids.

Um…what? Do I even have twenty-five friends? I could not believe it. And somehow, the groom mustered up twenty-five reluctant groomsmen to pair perfectly with each woman. But the craziness did not end there, as each of the twenty-five bridesmaids were wearing white, floor-length gowns. They all looked like mini brides. I honestly could not tell which one was getting married. It was like she was making the guests play a guessing game. It was Where's Waldo, wedding edition, but she wasn't standing out by wearing a red striped sweater and hipster glasses.

But it gets better - each of the gowns, all different except for the unifying theme of white, were also risqué, to say the least. I could safely say I would be embarrassed to wear any of them in front of my grandparents. The worst was a completely backless white silk gown that dipped down so low the woman wearing it was practically mooning everyone. It showed more cleavage than Pamela Anderson on her worst day, complete with a gaudy rhinestone belt buckle. Most of the other dresses fell along these same revealing and gaudy lines.

They all lined up to begin their entrance into the ceremony. At that point, I still could not differentiate which woman was actually the one about to tie the knot, as they all blended together into a mass of white silk, fake books and teased hair.

Finally, the twenty-five bridesmaids and groomsmen started to walk down the aisle, one by one. Fifteen minutes later, finally they are all standing up front. There were so many bodies crammed in the front of the ballroom that they started spilling out into the side aisle, making just one big cluster of wedding party.

Finally, when they are all settled into some sort of formation, the orchestra changed their tune, and the guests rose and turned to watch the bride walk down the aisle. I mean, they could only assume the one girl left standing in the hallway was the bride, but at that point, anything was possible. She began her trek down the aisle towards her groom, who was hiding somewhere within the mass of tuxedoed groomsmen, and I was almost more shocked at what she was wearing than the dresses of her bridesmaids. One would think that because every one of her twenty-five bridesmaids were wearing white, floor-length gowns, this bride would try to up the ante a bit on her own, so she stood out from the rest. Perhaps a massive, hot pink frock and a crown with fireworks shooting out of it or something, anything to distinguish her from the others. Well, she didn't. She was just wearing a plain white, strapless gown that had little to no poof at the bottom, and her hair was slicked back into a bun. Her outfit was so anti-climactic that I fell asleep for three seconds while looking at it.

After the bride entered, Pam scuttled over and quietly shut the heavy wooden doors of the ballroom, glared at me just because she could, and told me to go get ready for the reception. I was glad to put down the heavy metal yarmulke tray and go scour the kitchen for food to steal. I left, but my mind still lingered in amazement on the weirdest wedding party I had ever seen. Let's just hope the new husband knew which bride to kiss at the alter. Mazel tov.

Aretha Franklin – Up Close and Really, Really Personal

Yes, you just read that title correctly. Let me explain. I overheard this amazing story while working, and it is too good not to pass on.

A Palm Beach socialite at a function I was working was casually talking to one of her other fancy friends. She was wearing her tightest little black dress. Her lips were overly plumped, perhaps with fat taken from her butt, which was unusually taut and lifted for a woman of her age. Her hair was bigger than that of a Texan woman's in a windstorm, and her stilettos were so tall they could easily be used to grill a shish kabob. I always look for those big, overly teased coifs and try and listen in to their attached human's conversation. The way I figure it, the more time a woman spends on ratting out her roots, the more likely she will be to do other weird activities that are worth eavesdropping on. And besides, tuning in to the tales of other people's lives was much more entertaining than watching the same band sing the same Lady Gaga songs over and over again, and much more calorie friendly then shoving bacon-wrapped scallops in my mouth behind a curtain. And this particular evening I was especially glad I eavesdropped, as this treat of a tale was what wafted into my ears:

Big Hair LBD Woman:

"So, I was at this movie premier the other day in L.A. Everyone was there, it was hot. We started taking our seats in these long rows of

chairs, you know…it was a movie theater. I was trying to sit down without ripping my skintight mini, when all of a sudden, Aretha Franklin comes and sits right at the end of our row! Aretha freaking Franklin. We were all star struck… but then we realized… we were also all STUCK! Love her, but the woman is big and to go around her would be a feat. Especially in my new five-inch Christian Loubouitans and skirt.

So the movie begins, and about a half hour into it some people sitting a few seats down from me got up to use the restroom, as we all just spent the last hour shoving as many free martinis down our throats as our livers could bear, so a little tinkle action was bound to happen. When they got up, they looked around to weigh their exit strategy options. Option one: walk all the way down this huge, long row, waving their liposuctioned butts in front of everyone's faces and likely trip on their feet. OR! Option two… a short route that ends with a climb over mount Aretha. Both the ladies acted like chickens and took the long route. But when I had to use the ladies room, I saw how everyone had made a fool of themselves walking down the entire row, and I was not about to do the same. I decided to be brave, and take on the Aretha. So, I walked a couple seats over and I said … "Miss Aretha. I mean no dis- R.E.S.P.E.C.T, but I need to get out. And there is no way but up and over yo' big ole self!"

And she said to me in her deep voice "Baby, if you can get over me, more power to ya!"

And so I hiked up my mini skirt and try to work my way around her. I had cleared one thigh when I realized that I was stuck between her stomach and the chairs. I was in a full straddle with the queen of soul. My skirt is hiked up so high at this point my Hanky Panky's were showing. Gawd, it was even inappropriate for L.A.

So Aretha looked at me with a little twinkle in her eye and belts out 'I have never loved a man the way I love you.' And then… 'you make me feel like a natural woman. Wommannnnn.' So I shoot back, 'It isn't, it wasn't, it ain't never gonna be,' and I managed to wiggle my way past her."

As a child, we used to play this game on the playground called "spider," where you and a friend would sit face to face on a swing with your legs wrapped around each other. Looking back, it is painful to realize how incredibly sexual and just plain weird that "spider" position really is. Well this big haired socialite played spider with Aretha Franklin. She sat there face to face, legs wrapped around the queen of soul, shooting lyrics back and forth. Eventually she made it over the human road block, and the big world kept on turning. Aretha got a little love, and the woman got another story she could put in the safe under her pompadour. The LBD woman made a human bridge over troubled water.

Shady Politicians, Red Meat and Country Music.
God Bless America.

Every few months it seems a new government sex scandal hits the media. Is anyone even surprised anymore? It almost is a job requirement these days to have some sort of sketchy indignity under your belt if you want to be a well-known political figure. But it's not so often you see a scandal that hasn't yet been hit by the spotlight unfold before your eyes, unless you happen to work at a five-diamond hotel in the wealthiest town in America like I do so…yeah.

This is yet another story I wish I didn't have to witness, but I did. There was a cheap, (for Palm Beach, anyway), and poorly decorated function in one of our largest ballrooms. It was a dinner and meeting about something important, and to be honest, boring. Beige tablecloths covered the tables, no flower arrangements were at their center, and there was no music except for the cheesy hotel soundtrack that floated in through the ceiling speakers. When we whip out those tan tablecloths from the basement, it is an instant warning that the event is going to be about as exciting as your Mom's second cousin Edna's seventy-fifth birthday party, minus the free food.

But while the inside of the ballroom was about as hopping as jury duty, the outside was a little more exciting. The hallways were riddled with huge, thick-necked secret service men, wearing all black with their American flag lapel pins glinting in the overhead lights. A senator was the guest that night, and those men were on a mission to keep him safe and sound like a prize-winning pig at the South Dakota state fair. Good thing they were there, because we all know how dangerous Palm Beach really is, with its 30 MPH speed limit and gray haired population.

Now for the sake of this senator's career and political integrity, he shall remain nameless. That, and the fact I actually forgot his name. But this particular mystery man was about sixty-five or seventy years old. He had white hair and was dressed in a navy blue pin-striped suit, also sporting the flag lapel pin, as any real American would. Sitting next to him at the table was his wife.

My friend and tuxedo comrade Tony drew the short stick and was chosen to serve the senator's table for the evening. Tony is Italian, has long, dark hair slicked into a low ponytail, olive skin, a good sense of humor, and used to serve in the Army. He was well liked in our employee community, always cracking a joke at the right time to break the tension, or impressing us with his gallant stories from Afghanistan.

It was early in the evening and we had just begun the reception. Tony was circling around his tables with a plate of cocktail wieners. Tony offered him an hors d'oeuvre, and the senator accepted. Just then, he grabbed Tony's arm and pulled him in close... real close. The senator whispered to Tony through his sly, yellow-toothed grin, "I like your smile." With a glance at Tony's nametag he crooned, "Tony."

"Ah... thank you?" a creeped-out Tony replied.

The senator tightened his grip on Tony's bicep, still firmly muscled from his stint oversees, and pulled him in even closer.

"No, son, I don't think you understand. I *really* like your smile."

And with that, he popped the cocktail wiener into his mouth, gave Tony a wink, and walked back over to his wife.

His poor, poor wife.

Tony, after nearly gagging, came right back to the kitchen and told us his horrifying tale. We all choked on the sushi rolls we were shoving in our mouths in the back freezer.

Kyle began laughing so hard stolen Sprite shot out of his nostrils.

At first I didn't believe Tony completely, but I kept a close eye on the political pervert for the rest of the night. I saw Senator Creepball gaze longingly in Tony's direction, or flash those yellowed chompers at him in a terrifying grin. All while his wife kept chatting, kept sipping her extra dirty martinis, and kept looking the other way. Perhaps this was how she survived most of her days, by looking the other way and numbing herself one cocktail at a time.

That was so disgusting. Good thing this man has the fate of our country in his hands. Sigh. Just another day on the job.

Pantie Perv

One thing that comes along with every job is weird co-workers. No matter where you work, or how awesome your job is, it is guaranteed there will be at least one lunatic working alongside you. You are thinking of the person at your office right now, aren't you?

At the hotel, we work with people from every different culture imaginable. It is pretty cool. I pass the time by asking my co-workers about their home countries and have learned a lot. Did you know it is rude for women in Jamaica to whistle? But it is perfectly acceptable for men. Whenever I would whistle every Jamaican woman in earshot would scold me and tell me to cut it out. Dude, I just had Lady Gaga stuck in my head… relax. I also love learning little snippets of their native tongue. I can swear and call someone ugly in five different languages. Just call me educated.

I work with so many people from so many places it often gets hard to keep track. Plus, often I will get people from out of department picking up a shift, or I will work as a hostess for a night in another department, things like that. It gets really hard remembering who I have worked with or met. This lack of recognition is especially evident when I run into some co-workers outside of work, when they don't have their little gold-plated nametags on. I have been approached in the grocery store and, not recognizing the person right away, throw out a "Oh… hey… you!" like a big idiot. It is one of these moments I will now share with you, dear reader.

I was in a department store shopping for some lingerie. My sister was getting married and I was buying her some hot little numbers to give to her at her bridal shower, which I was hosting that evening. My cart was piled high with unmentionables. For a split second, I turned to look at a rack of bras. When I turned back to my cart, a man was standing there with this tiny, cheetah-print thong I had picked out, and was tenderly stroking the crotch of it.

I gasped. (Side note-I just threw up remembering this moment.)

With mischievous eyes, he muttered, "How's your husband?" as he continued to stroke the panties.

What?! Who was this strange man stroking the thong that now should be burned? And how did he know my husband? I was terrified.

And then it hit me. Co-worker. Got it. I remembered him; he helped me serve shrimp one night. Hey there, person I can't remember your name and don't recognize you if you are not wearing a tux. Hey, how you doing…now get your nasty fingers off my lingerie. BARF.

I grabbed the underwear and replied with a short, "Fine, thanks," then turned and hurried away. Then I went in a corner and cried a little. Every time he sees me he probably thinks of that little underwear and the feel of it between his nasty digits. Gross. This is the only time I am grateful we wear a baggy polyester tuxedo coverall.

Ew. End of story.

No Sir, I Don't Want to Smoke Pot With You. Caviar?

Networking is a skill that we all have learned working in such a high-end environment. You never know what contacts you can make. Many times I won't even realize who I am chatting with as I casually make my waitress small talk. I will have full conversations with guests, only to have my supervisor tell me that person I was talking to was an African prince, or a washed out celebrity from thirty years ago. These people are generally to be regarded at a different level than the rest of us "normal folks." These people are "somebody."

This attitude of people falling into class systems does not sit well with me. Yes, someone may have more money than me, or be better known, but in all honestly, I could care less. My friend's lunatic dad with the crazy, mayonnaise-catching mustache said it best. When my friend and I were discussing this snotty classmate who was acting all high and mighty, he said: "Everyone poops the same way." Despite the hairy beast festering beneath his nostrils, he is still capable of producing random nuggets of wisdom. Who knew a sentence involving feces could change my life? But it is so true, so wise, so gross, but so right. Point of the story - it takes a lot for me to be intimidated by someone's celebrity. Dorkily excited to meet them, yes, as evidenced in a few previous stories. But kissing their designer shoes and bending over backwards to meet their every request – no thank you. However, I will try to rub some of their status and wealth off onto myself, in a desperate hope of advancing my career past the status of "waitress."

Kyle was serving one day, and making polite, five star quality conversation with his guests. One of the men at his table was particularly chatty. He had gray hair combed perfectly over to the side of his head and a little bald spot visible underneath. He wore khaki pants with green lobsters embroidered all over them, and these weird shoes rich people wear that actually are just slippers with their initials embroidered on them with gold thread. Hey, if I was rich and lived on an island I would probably wear weird slipper shoes as well.

The lobster pants slipper man began prying into Kyle's life. "Young man, what do you do besides shove food under rich peoples noses?"

"I am in college, studying to be an actor," Kyle replied.

"An actor! By golly! I have a house in Manhattan and know quite a few people up there. Maybe I could set you up with someone. Here is my card," Lobster Pants said. Kyle, of course, graciously accepted the business card. It was very classy and professional on thick cardstock. It simply said the man's name, his phone number, then beneath in elegant script *Manhattan* and *Palm Beach.*[19]

Kyle came back into the kitchen where I was about to enter the cooler to steal a cool, crisp Perrier water. "Katie, this guy at my table is being weirdly friendly. He knows a lot of people in New York, and gave me his business card. Basically, I am already famous."

"Sweet, dude. I will start writing your Oscar acceptance speech," I said, and began picking at a cheese plate, which is always a risky endeavor. Do I really know how long that cheese has been sitting out? No, but I will always risk my health for free Brie.

Kyle returned to his tables to fill up water glasses (they must never go below the three-fourths full line. It is one of our standards. People probably think we are crazy: they take two sips

---

[19] I hope I can have such a classy business card one day. As of now, it would say "Katie: tuxedo-wearing, Toyota-driving server who likes cats. Address: A cockroach-ridden apartment on the mainland." Sigh.

and we are right there to re-fill, but, hey, that's what we do in fine dining - we care about your hydration.) Mr. Lobster Pants Slipper Shoes apparently was still in a chatty mood. He gestured for Kyle to approach him again. "Hey, are you working tomorrow night?"

Kyle, hoping the man would say, "because I got you this great audition," or, "I want you to meet my friend, this super awesome movie producer," replied earnestly, "No, sir!"

"Oh! Well, I am having a party at my house down the road. You and your wife should come!" Invited to a Palm Beach party, thrown by an old rich man in expensive slippers? I could only imagine the delicious snacks that would be served. Many of my activities are centered on whether free food will be involved. If there is, I am ninety-five percent more likely to attend. Kyle thanked the man for the offer, and continued to fill up the water glasses that were practically full anyway.

He found me in the back as I was shoving the most fattening in the world-mashed potatoes into my mouth while crouching behind a stack of chairs. Kyle dished about the party invite. I thought it was a little sketchy, yet intriguing. I instantly began mentally scanning my closet for something that would be even semi-Palm Beach worthy. Kyle took two bites of my amazing mashed potatoes, and we both headed back out to our tables.

Again, for a third time, the Lobster Pants Palm Beacher gestured Kyle over, this time pulling him in uncomfortably close. So close Kyle could see a fleck of asparagus stuck to the man's dry lips. Lobster Pants threw Kyle a little wink and hoarsely whispered, "Do you smoke a J? Come over and we can get hiiigghhh!" He let out a terrible old man cackle right in Kyle's face, his breath smelling like whiskey and death.

Ah, it all made sense now. Why did we not see this earlier? A classy, Palm Beach businessman wanted us youthful college kids to come over and be his drug buddies. Clearly the first thing I think of when I see a respectable, pulled together Palm Beach man wearing yacht clothes and driving a Jag is "wow, what a stoner he must be."

Poor Kyle had to decline his request, in the overly polite, professional tone we use with guests. "Ah, no sir, I do not use, um... J's, but I guess, ah... thank you for the offer?" Cue the awkward turtle.

So instead of Kyle getting an excellent New York City contact, all of his networking efforts resulted in him getting a really rich buddy he can watch *Harold and Kumar Go to White Castle* with and pig out on gourmet Cheetos while channeling his inner Bob Marley. The only thing that sounds appealing about that to me is gourmet Cheetos. Yum.

Fish Fetus is Not Fine Dining

Listen up kids, I need to vent about something. Working at a five-diamond resort on the wealthiest island in the world, I have served some weird, fancy-schmancy food. It never ceases to amaze me how a slimy, fatty liver or something that is popped out of a fish's uterus can be considered a delicacy. I want to discuss three foods I think are absolutely disgusting, but still cost more than a week of groceries. If you truly want to be a person of dignity and class, please get with the program and see how disgusting these three things are. Then, go pig out on guacamole and cheese dip and call it a night.

1. Caviar.

I love how at parties I will carry around trays of something absolutely delicious, such as a mini Cuban sandwich, and nobody wants to eat it. Buttery bread, ham, melted Swiss cheese, spicy brown mustard and a cute little pickle slice, all perfectly toasted into a mini piece of heaven. Delectable. Decadent. Scrumptious. However, people turn their noses at the sight of a tiny bit of calorific bliss, worrying their lipo-suctioned thighs will revert back to their old jiggly ways.

But then I will bring around a huge tub of dark forest green, slimy, stinky caviar, and the tables turn. (When I serve it I almost want to speak in a British accent; it just seems more appropriate. "Would you care for some caviar?" A British accent is so much better than a Minnesotan one. If I were offering tuna casserole it would be a whole different story.) When I have caviar, I suddenly become more than the annoying girl with the fuzzy blonde hair and necktie, and I transform into super waitress of the century. Everybody wants to be my best friend and sit next to me on the school bus. When I offer the tub of gooey fish eggs, everyone begins acknowledging that I am indeed a human being, and they light up with excitement over the mass of slimy minnow fetuses resting on my silver tray. *"Oh, caviar! Delicious! How lovely. I adore caviar."* Blah blah blah. Really? You really love this? Are you sure you are not just putting on a fish-egg-loving front for Pretentious Polly sitting at your right? If you pass on the caviar, you risk the chance of looking "low class." So, because of its predetermined status, the caviar always sells.

Of course, everybody knows caviar is actually fish eggs. However, for the purpose of emphasizing my distaste for the so-called delicacy, I did a Google search to see what *type* of fish it actually comes from. Let's just say, it is no cute little finding Nemo, rather a hybrid of a demon and Hulk Hogan, otherwise known as sturgeon. While there are several different types of sturgeons, all of them are equally terrifying. Their facial structures alone make me want to never enter the ocean again, let alone eat their unborn young. Some sturgeons have these huge, nasty, catfish-like mustaches hanging from their boney mouths. Any fish that sports a mustache is not okay with me, and should not be consumed in any stage of its life, whether it is egg or full-blown adult. No, thank you. With an abundance of food options to choose from, I'd pass on the caviar and stick with the veggie tray.

2.   Foie Gras.

For anyone not accustomed to the weird language of fine dining, I will translate foie gras. It is French for 'fatty liver.' That alone should turn you off, but let me continue. To make foie gras, you first take a duck and strap it into a tiny cell and feed it until it wants to explode. Once it begins to resemble Michael Moore, it is ready for the killing. With a little slice and dice, take out the liver, slap in on a cracker and top it with whatever you feel like. At the hotel, we often serve it topped with - brace yourself - peanut butter and jelly. I just threw up a little writing that. It's a far stretch from the PB&J my mom would pack me back in the good old days for school lunch. At what point in life do we stop wanting peanut butter and jelly on delicious white Wonder bread and instead turn to fatty duck liver? People of France, I love and adore you, and had a delightful trip to Paris last summer, but I will pass on the foie gras, and instead opt for the Nutella crepe.

3. The Oyster.

I know oysters are not that fancy, or even that gross. People enjoy them in fine dining restaurants or at a skanky little seafood joint on a pier in Virginia Beach. However, slurping down something that has the consistency of a slimly lymph node is not appealing to me, especially when it smells like a marina on crack. But there's a reason I added the oyster to the list of foods I won't eat no matter how dignified I become. A lovely gentleman who works at the hotel carting dirty dishes down into the dishwashing room told me this tale of oyster horror. Since he gets to encounter all the leftover food (and trust me, there always is enough to feed every homeless person in Florida), he always makes himself a plate for dinner before dumping it all into the trash. He told me he loved oysters, and whenever a raw bar would come through he would eat a couple. Then, one night, he cracked opened the shell. Inside, instead of a delicious sea muscle, there was a worm. This parasitical creature had consumed the entire oyster before any human even had a chance. That is just disgusting. So ladies, wear those pearls to the party, but pass on their shelled creator, unless you want to risk consuming something that resembles a mini version of a Graboid from the 1990's flick *Tremors*. I love you Kevin Bacon.

Take this as a lesson on how to truly eat with class and dignity at a high society event. Politely say "no thank you" when offered the eggs of a giant, mustache-wielding fish, or worm-eaten oysters, and say "yes please" to the hummus platter and mini cheeseburgers. Yum!

Bootylicious Socialite

This night's shift was a huge charity event we have every year at the hotel. Our most beautiful ballroom was decorated all in white – very classy and very Palm Beach. All the socialites were in attendance and dressed in their very finest. The silk was flowing; the intricate beading was sparkling in the light. Hair was elegantly wrapped in French twists, freshly blown out from the Edward Beauty Salon. The men's tuxedos were new and wrinkle-free, the ties and pocket squares loud with color and patterns, in true Palm Beach style. It was cocktail hour, and the Frank Sinatra wanna-be was crooning all the classics.

I went back into the kitchen to bring out a plate of sushi, always a crowd pleaser on such a weight-conscious island. As I re-entered the ballroom, I could sense something was different. The aura of the room had shifted. I noticed several ladies' eyes kept darting to a corner of the room. The tone of the party was quiet, people whispering little comments before sipping their martinis and rolling their eyes. I followed their glances and I instantly saw what everyone in the room had already discovered.

A Palm Beach gent had entered the room, grabbed some champagne and began his mingle session like all the rest. Attached to his arm was his date, a beautiful white woman, her lips plumped and her hair bleached blonde, clearly accustomed to the ways of the island. However, the Palm Beach Princess had on a very peculiar outfit. The socialite looked like she just walked out of a hip-hop club from the sketchiest party of Clematis Street. The woman was dressed… ghetto. There was no other way to describe it. While the rest of the Palm Beach ladies were in floor-length gowns and vintage jewels, she chose to wear booty shorts and a belly chain, which until that moment I thought had become extinct sometime around 1995. She had on big hoop earrings that had the word 'phresh' written in rhinestones across their centers. Her lipstick was bright red, her shorts were branded Apple Bottom and her midriff T-shirt read "Sexy Mama." She wore black boots that went up past her knees with stiletto heels that could kill someone in a fight. Her blond hair was braided into corn rows. Yes, corn rows. On Palm Beach. Usually the only corn rows on the island are hair tracks covered by long, perfectly blonde hair extensions. Someone alert the media, this was a first in the history of the island.

It was so obvious that everyone was staring and whispering about the woman. I almost choked on the tense air. But the urban elephant in the room didn't care, or didn't seem to notice the world staring at her. The room became hushed as the Palm Beach socialite gone ghetto walked up to the band to request a song. All eyes were on her and her ridiculously short shorts as she walked over to the stage to talk to the band leader. What song did she request? Why, Fergilicious, of course. The song began blaring from the speakers, and she put down her apple Martini, squealing in delight as she pulled her man to the dance floor.

Watching Palm Beachers dance is always entertaining and slightly nauseating at the same time. Picture how terrible it is when your mom or grandma hit the dance floor with moves so embarrassing they should be put up on YouTube. Now imagine those same terrible dance moves backed by years and years of waltzing lessons from Daddy's country club. Couples prance and gallop across the floor with stiff smiles on their Botoxed faces, their backs perfectly erect as if wearing a neck brace.

However, the ghetto socialite was far from fox trotting, and it was clear she did not learn her moves from ballroom class, but from taking too many Zumba classes. She spread her legs, put her hands on her hips, and moved them in a way never before attempted on the island. She was popping it and locking it, and I was losing it. My mouth dropped in shock, and my tray almost followed. It took all I had not to die laughing right then and there.

But then, a Palm Beach miracle happened. Another couple walked onto the dance floor, and started bumping and grinding like it was nobody's business. Laughter flitted through the air as the tension broke, and more couples headed to the dance floor to get down and dirty. By the time the next song started, the ballroom looked like my middle school homecoming dance (a memory I prefer not to think about). This hip-hopping Palm Beach socialite had gotten the party started, and kept it going all night long. People were laughing, dancing, sweating in their stiff gowns and suit coats. The dance floor was packed the entire night and the band was belting out all the latest pop hits. Perhaps by the end of the evening, all the socialites would have forgotten about the woman and her booty shorts and corn rows, and wouldn't even remember to gossip about it over Bloody Mary's in the morning. Doubtful. But if the ghetto woman had enough confidence to walk into the hotel wearing hot pants and stiletto boots, who knows what else she could do. The woman was fierce, and I applauded her for her zest.

Wait, Did You Just Grab His Johnson?

Hopefully this story is more fun to read than it was to experience. Cue disgusted shuddering. This story haunts my dreams, lurks near me in shadowy corners and spends most of the winter months hiding under my bed like a festering old childhood monster. That may have been a little melodramatic, but that is the kind of mood I am in so deal with it. Read on if you think you can stomach a tale of extremely creepy Palm Beach behavior.

Setting: Big fundraiser banquet. Me: Tuxedo clad, serving wine. It was one of those boring shifts when the only thing I really had to do was walk around, fold napkins, and try and overhear entertaining bits of conversation. On shifts like these, small talk with guests can often be the ticket to a semi-interesting evening.

I refilled the water glass of a guest at my table. He was middle aged, balding, and wearing a chocolate brown suit with a faded tie. He said hello, and began initiating small talk. He asked if I was in school, and I told him I was. Kyle walked by just then, and I pointed at him and said he was my husband, and was an actor. The balding man became excited because his son, who was about our age, was also an actor. So we began chatting about the actors union, New York City, and all those other trivial topics you speak of when you really only have one thing in common. This mindless chatter was more entertaining than walking around with heavy bottles of wine, so I was glad for the diversion.

Now, let me make this crystal clear. The bald man and I were talking about my *husband*. That meant I was a married woman. In a committed relationship. Taken. Off the market. Not a threat. And even if I were single, I mean come on. The man was fifty! And obviously if I was going to be a gold digger, the man should at least be sixty-five or seventy. And he was talking about his young adult *son*. That meant he was the father to a guy that was the same age as me. You get the picture. There was nothing sketchy about our small talk conversation. Nada. However, this chat of utmost innocence apparently sparked a flame of jealousy within the depths of his wife. She was sitting right next to him, her blonde, curly hair in a puff on top of her head, secured with a black scrunchie.[20] As the bald man and I continued our innocent conversation, I noticed the wife casually looked around, then reached her perfectly manicured red nails over to her husband's lap and started groping his crotch. She fiddled his diddle. Tickled his pickle. Whatever you want to call it – this lady got a little freaky with the man I was currently engaging in polite conversation with. Apparently, she had thought her little plan of seductive action was hidden under the tablecloth, but as fate would have it, the man had just scooted his chair back from the table to better position himself to talk to me, and his lap was in the wide open air of the ballroom for all to see. I had a front row seat to this little perv session.

When the wife made the initial contact with the man's crown jewels he twitched, obviously shocked by the woman's immediate need to express her control issues… I mean, love. After a brief glance down to his lap, by both of us, we both just pretended like it never happen, forcing our conversation to continue as if neither of us noticed the groping session happening right before our eyes. But then, as I was desperately looking for a way to get out of there FAST, her happy hands went back for more, still oblivious that her husband's lap was

---

[20] Why do people still wear scrunchies? There is no excuse for such outdated hair apparel. All scrunchies should be sentenced to a life of dusty dollar store shelf demise.

not, in fact, hiding under the tablecloth, but was rather uncovered for all to see.

I decided to act cool and pretend like I didn't see round two of the grope fest. "Ahh… um… yeah… my husband loves theater… ah… Shakespeare… hooo boy. Okay… any more wine? Okay, great… nice talk, bye." And with that, I scooted back into the kitchen. There was no graceful way to get out of a situation like that.

Later in the evening, I saw the balding man and the nutcase wife talking in a low, stern tone, clearly having a married couple fight and trying to conceal it by whispering. I didn't refill either of their wine glasses the rest of the evening. SICK.

Hors d'oeuvres? Oh My Gosh, Boobs.

In the middle of the hotel is a courtyard, where we often hold receptions or breakfasts on steamy South Florida summer mornings. To set up for a breakfast, we have to sometimes get to work at 4:30 a.m. The heat is already sweltering and by the time the guests get there it looks like they are being served by a clan of frizzy haired homeless people who haven't slept for days. But despite being riddled with sweaty servers, the courtyard is elegant and beautiful, with huge staircases on all sides pointing toward a central fountain, complete with classical Greek statues spitting water out of their little circular stone mouths. The ground is covered in crooked, old cobblestone bricks, which provide an excellent opportunity to trip and fall on your face, but that's another story. Guest rooms surround the courtyard, and light up at night like fire flies in the tropical sky.

Let me give you the run down for this evening. Party: Hoity-toity Reception. Time of day: Night. Rooms around the courtyard: Illuminated. We were tuxedoed and ready to get the good times rolling. I grabbed a plate of mini cheeseburgers, usually a crowd pleaser even to the men and women who are watching their figure. I mean, who can resist a perfect little cheeseburger the size of a silver dollar? With my mouth already slightly salivating over my own pending cheeseburger consumption, I entered the courtyard to begin my night of tuxedo slavery.

As soon as I got outside and descended the crooked stone steps, I noticed something very weird was going on. All the male servers, and even some of the women, were walking around with their heads tilted slightly back, their faces cast upward as if trying to get a nocturnal tan. They were hardly even looking at the guests as they offered them food and drinks, rather their eyes were permanently gazing upward at some unknown object. I meandered over to my co-worker Olaf, a tall, beefy Jamaican man. He has a thick accent that makes me want to play my favorite Bob Marley CD every time he opens his mouth. Olaf, too, had his eyes fixed upward. "Olaf," I said, waving my gloved hand in front of his face. "What's up… literally?"

Olaf replied with a single word: *"Boobs."* Boobs? I followed his gaze, and there, high in the sky hovering over the courtyard, was, indeed, a pair of boobs. Some wonderfully intelligent guest had decided to get ready for her big, glamorous night out completely naked, in front of a window, and with ever light on in the room. Her entire nude silhouette was visible to a courtyard full of people wining and dining. We could see everything. And, being a woman getting ready for a night out on Palm Beach, she had to look her best. It is not easy being beautiful! So, she stayed there, naked and visible, for almost an hour. A couple of the male servers at that point positioned themselves off to the side with their hands behind their backs, looking very professional and official, as if they were there for some very important purpose, but in reality they were watching a free peep show. Disgusting.

Finally, after about an hour and a half, Ms. Nude flicked off the lights and went into another room to slip on her gown and head out on the town, seemingly unaware that hundreds of people now knew that she had a large red birthmark on her left butt cheek. You should never know that about a stranger, but I, and about 200 others, now do. Please, people of the world, remember to shut your blinds while prancing around in your birthday suit. We will all benefit.

Political Conjugal[21]

I am not a democrat. Nor am I a republican. I don't even think I am an independent for that matter – don't judge me for my lack of a political affiliation. What I am is a twenty–something critical thinker who, during election time, takes an educated look at all available options and tries desperately not to be deceived by the media and dramatic political advertisements. Then, I use my brain to make an intelligent decision as to who I would think would be the best candidate for the available office, and I carefully cast my vote. Very carefully, as we in Palm Beach County desperately do not want a repeat of the 2000 hanging chad incident. If I hear the words hanging chad one more time in my life, it will be one too many. Who came up with the term 'hanging chad,' anyway? That is what is wrong with American politics: the words hanging chad. Or even just chad, for that matter. These words are like the cockroach of the English language- useless and disgusting.

Now that we have established my strong distaste for cockroaches and chads, and that I am not a loud mouth republican, nor do I have a faded "Mama's for Obama" bumper sticker on my Toyota, we can proceed with the story. Conservative radio show host Rush Limbaugh lives in Palm Beach, so naturally, when he wants to have a little get together, he rents out a massive ballroom at the hotel and throws a party that costs more than the healthcare reform bill. As I arrived at my shift that evening, Craig, in a quiet voice and with a piece of

---

[21] Whoa…conjugal? I will never say wedding again. Thanks thesaurus.

spinach very visible on his left front tooth, gathered all the servers in a corner.

"Listen up, everyone," he began in a sharp whisper. The spinach didn't move a centimeter. "This is a triple VIP event tonight. It is Mr. Limbaugh's birthday party, and his guest list is packed full famous and powerful people, so get it together and no mistakes." With a strong emphasis on the 'S' in mistakes, the fleck of spinach flew off Craig's tooth and vanished from sight. After being momentarily distracted by the flying foliage, I became extremely excited about the night's pending celebrity adventure. Rush Limbaugh in all his glory was about to waltz through the heavy wooden ballroom doors, and was bringing all of his besties along with him. Every republican who has ever appeared on or hosted a Fox News show would be bumping and grinding in our midst in a matter of hours. I was so excited. Again, not because I was a devout republican, but because usually I was just serving ninety-year-old ladies in ugly designer gowns. A room of celebrities, whoever they may be, is far more exciting.

Rush did not hold back one bit on his party expenditures. The room was dressed lavishly, with more flowers than in the White House rose garden. Each table was covered with expensive rented fine china and glassware. In the center of each plate lay a blue metallic box, tied with a pretty ribbon. Inside was a piece of white chocolate, with Rush's signature written across it in some type of edible ink. I never knew that chocolate could become so political, but I was indeed staring at the single most republican piece of candy in the nation.

Soon the crowd started pouring in. Mike Huckabee was there, having recently been ousted from the 2008 presidential election. I felt like I should pour him a whisky to take the edge off that one. Maybe next time buddy, maybe next time.

Then a tall, leggy and loudmouthed blonde made her way through the double doors: Anne Coulter. She was wearing a dark purple bandage dress with black platform pumps, her hair down and as stick straight as always, with an abundant amount of dark shadow rimming her icy eyes. The chick is fierce, on camera and off. She looked even taller and skinnier in person, especially with those five-inch stilettos on. She reminded me of a baby giraffe clunking around the African planes. Either that, or a lanky, terrifying alien. "Take me to your conservatives," I expected her to say, shooting a laser gun at a picture of President Obama.

I went up and offered her a drink, and I will admit it was not because I was concerned about her thirst, but because I just wanted an excuse to talk to her.[22]

Ready to hear what she ordered? This is exciting … drum roll please …she got a Diet Coke with no ice. No ice! That is absolutely sick. Our Diet Coke comes in dusty glass bottles and is stored in a warm room of the basement. Sick. Please use ice. But apparently she loved the Coke in all its lukewarm glory, and ordered about forty-five more that evening. I guess her key to being skinny is to have a constant stream of caffeine and artificial sweetener running through her veins.

The ballroom was full and the republicans were partying hard (in their own conservative way, of course), when the man of the evening made his grand entrance. Somebody please blow a trumpet or shoot confetti in the air, because Rush Limbaugh had arrived. He busted through the double doors, surrounded by a posse of ten. He made his way through the crowd, stopping every two steps to shake a hand and make small talk. I again saw this as a great opportunity to use my waitress powers to force my way into the lives of the rich and famous. I was guessing that Rush was not a 'Diet Coke, no ice' type of man, so I went into the kitchen, grabbed a plate of mini cheeseburgers, and made my way over to him. The man has to love red meat, right?

"Mr. Limbaugh, would you care for a cheeseburger in paradise[23]?" I asked. When Rush saw my plate of meat and

---

[22] I did the same with Matt Lauer at another party, but he was not so excited about my beverage offerings. He gave me a short, un-friendly 'no thanks' with a weird hand flip, and no eye contact. I was heartbroken. I am an aspiring journalist; I just wanted him to speak wisdom into my life. Sigh. I can never look at *The Today Show* the same way, despite how peppy Savannah Guthrie attempts to be.

cheese, his face lit up like a kid in a cupcake store. He oohed and ahhed, then shoved two in his mouth at once, just as I expected.

Rush and his gaggle of geese around him ended up cleaning off my cheeseburger plate, until there was nothing left but small pools of grease and half of a mini hamburger bun from the woman who was "trying to watch her carbs."

With my plate empty except for the stupid half of a bun, I left the ballroom and made a bee line for the kitchen to load up my plate with more excuses to talk to famous people. As I turned the corner, I saw Craig backed up against the wall as a guest screamed at him, her arms flailing in the air with rage. She had badly ratted hair (1989 is long gone, let your bangs lay flat, people!) and was wearing a ho-hum, mother of the bride dress that had too much taffeta shoved under the skirt. I was curious as to what could have made this woman so upset. Did Craig kidnap her first-born child? Did he con her out of all her finances, Bernie Madoff style? I had to know, so I jumped into extreme eavesdropping mode to get my answer.

"Republicans... REPUBLICANS!" The woman yelled. "How could you allow a group of such DISGUSTING creatures into this hotel on the day of my daughter's WEDDING!"

Ooohhh, we have an angry liberal on our hands. Watch out, everyone.

"This is absolutely absurd," she continued. "I will NOT have my daughter walking past this room full of pure EVIL on the day of her HOLY MATRIMONY!"

Just when I thought I had heard it all, that woman graced my life with her presence. Now, I understand if you strongly dislike republicans, or democrats, or anyone just annoyingly opinionated like Mr. Limbaugh. But to detest someone with opposite views as you, so much so that you find it necessary to

---

[23] They make us call them that, much to my embarrassment. What if Jimmy Buffet, another Palm Beacher, was there? I would feel incredibly foolish going up to him and offering him a mini meat patty named after his own lyrics. That would be like going up to Snoop Dog and offering him a Gin and Juice. It's just weird.

flip out on your daughter's wedding? Over the top. Someone get her a Xanax and a flat iron for those bangs.

But good old Craig, in his true five-star servant manner, remained calm. He cooed at her, tried to settle her down, and kept assuring her that her anger was completely justified, though in actuality she was acting completely insane. He then explained they would simply re-route the wedding party through the hotel, so they would never have to come within five feet of a Republican the entire evening. (Little did she know Craig was George Bush's biggest fan.) The woman finally calmed down and left, and I went back to passing out conversation starters to the rich and famous.

A half hour later I was in the hallway, on my way to the kitchen to get some elderly person a hot water with lemon, when I saw the liberal wedding party make their way down the hallways. The bridesmaids' dresses were dark blue, with rhinestone pictures of President Obama on their butts. Okay, obviously that is a lie – but I guarantee there is somebody out there in the world with an Obama dress. Yep, just did a Google search and there are tons. Oh what a fine, odd country we live in.

The Samurai Sensation

I have seen famous singers, 80's rock bands, and Cirque du Soleil performances at the hotel. I have seen firework displays, naked women painted gold (sick), and amazing magicians. The entertainment at the parties I am working always doubles as my entertainment for the evening, and that is one perk of being a Palm Beach waitress. However, no entertainment act excites me more than when they bring in the traditional Japanese drummers. (I know, I'm a dork.)

It is called Taiko drumming, and is truly amazing. The stage gets covered with huge drums, and a massive gong sits near the back. The drummers all dress in traditional Japanese clothing, but sometimes I secretly wonder if they are just wearing a silky bathrobe from Target. The Taiko group comes to the hotel quite often. Basically whenever someone orders a lot of sushi for a reception, they feel it is appropriate to have such drumming played in the background. I have no complaints, as I love the drums and I love sushi so it is a win-win.

Most of the drummers are Asian, but there always is the one little blonde girl that leaves me wondering how she got involved in such an extracurricular activity. And she also leaves me jealous, because instead of beating out all of my life's frustrations on a massive drum while wearing weird pajamas, I am standing in one spot for four hours at a time, offering champagne that I am not allowed to drink. But the best part of the drumming ceremony is not the blonde girl, nor the deafening beats. The best part is the Samurai warrior that comes with every performance.

This mysterious man dresses in traditional Samurai garb and prowls through the ballroom, massive sword and all in complete stealth. He has a helmet that flaps over his ears, and a flimsy Fu Manchu mustache that looks like something I once pulled out of my shower drain. His thick armor hangs over his shoulders and around his waist, I guess in case any of the guests tries to attack him with a butter knife. The best part, in my opinion, is that he even wears those Ninja Turtle-style socks under his traditional Japanese sandals. Amazing, oh Ninja Turtle sock man, you look absolutely amazing.

This "warrior" creature takes his job very seriously. He has walked right up to me before, staring me straight in the eye and holding his sword up like he was about to cut my arm off, his lips quivering in anger. Hopefully the anger part is acting, and not his true pent up aggression towards his job, because he is holding a weapon, and things could get feisty.

With the creepy warrior in our midst, I knew that night was going to be a lovely evening. The guests started to pour in, and the sushi was flying off the plates and conveniently into my mouth behind the closed doors of the kitchen. The room was humming with excitement, chatter, and Palm Beach gossip.

About a half hour into the reception, the drummers take their places and begin their rhythmic banging, their beats vibrating the glasses I was carrying on my tray. One particular woman in attendance at that party had already taken about five of the champagnes I had been passing around. Her lips were bigger than Goldie Hawn's, and her hair a few shades blonder. The skin on her face was stretched so tight it looked like the casing of a hot dog. Her dress was a floor-length yellow number that had more rhinestones and sequins on it than my high school dance costumes. The woman was Palm Beach fierce. She was talking so loudly out of her hot pink glossed lips that I could almost hear her clearly over the loud drumming. She was making huge motions with her arms, a little of her champagne spilling out of her glass with each syllable. She seemed oblivious to everything else except the little crowd she was entertaining with her stories and loud laughter. She was annoying.

The Samurai warrior suddenly appeared next to me. "Hello!" I said to him. I had seen him about ten times; we should have been practically best friends at that point. He glared at me and grunted. Man, that guy never broke character.

He too had spotted the bright yellow canary Palm-Beacher chirping in the middle of the crowd. He studied her for a minute as if planning a war strategy. His hand slowly and steadily reached for the sword that was hanging from his belt. His eyes were fixed on the woman in the annoying yellow dress. He swung his sword back over his shoulder, setting it at the perfect angle to decapitate someone at any moment. I was frightened. He began his quiet slow steps over toward the loud woman, each Ninja Turtle foot gingerly placed in front of the other with careful precision. That man was on a mission.

The warrior gets within inches of the loud woman, her back turned to him so she was completely unaware of the man with the nasty Fu Manchu lingering mere inches from the back of her neck. His slow, methodical breaths fluttered the woman's diamond chandelier earrings. People in her group obviously saw this warrior lurking behind the woman, but ignored him, their curiosity as to what was about to happen next keeping them quiet.

The warrior, with his face right behind the woman's ear, lifted his sword over his head and let out a loud, frightening war cry. "RAAAHAHHAHHAHAHAHAH," is how I can best dictate to you the ridiculous growl that escaped past his lips. Sound it out, people, sound it out.

The loud Palm Beacher screamed bloody murder at the startling cry behind her. Her champagne glass flew up into the air, the sticky liquid raining down on eight nearby guests. She whipped around to come face-to-face with her Samurai attacker, his sword still drawn over his head, and she fell to the ground in fright. The whole spectacle was amazing. The woman was lying flat on the floor in a puddle of champagne, embarrassment, and yellow sequined tulle.

The warrior lowered his arms, looked around with his sly Samurai eyes, put his sword back in position and took slow, careful steps right out of the ballroom. He never broke character, he never spoke a word, but he just left the sprawled out socialite on the ground in a pile of gown. Mission accomplished. I now realize why this man does what he does. He must love his job.

Bad Hair and Band-Aids

When I arrived at the hotel for an evening shift one night, I was quickly informed that the band Styx would be performing at dinner. Sweet! Who is Styx? I know, I know, shame on me for not being born yet when the band hit their rock and roll peak. But after forcing a couple co-workers to sing some lyrics, I recognized their musical genius. For all you fellow 1987'ers who may also draw a Styx blank, hit up the Google and you will immediately be transported back into a time of classic rock bliss. Cue the big hair, bell bottomed pants, leather jackets and disgusting mustaches. Really disgusting mustaches.

The band's crew was already busy setting up the stage when I got into the ballroom. The stage was massive, and the décor was classy. All of us tuxedo-wearing losers were working quickly to get our tables set up before the pending cocktail hour was set to begin.

About an hour later, guests started to arrive. With my black tie tied tight and my hair already a frizzy mess, I began to serve. And while I looked like a baby chimpanzee in a tux, the guests were dressed like movie stars. But a couple of minutes into the wine and dine session, I began to notice some people that just didn't look like they "fit in." These odd balls had hair just a little too long, and a touch too "business in the front party in the back" mulletesque. Instead of looking like Palm Beach class, you could see Zubaz sticking out of the bottoms of their pilling tuxedo pants. Basically, a couple of guys drifted in who looked exactly like that embarrassing photo of your uncle Billy at that college kegger back in 1982.[24] It seemed that these slightly aged ex-rock star wannabees had invaded the hotel in hopes of catching a free Styx show.

Just then Craig burst into the ballroom, his eyes narrowed and darting about. It appeared someone tipped him off about the mullet invaders, and he was not going to stand for it. He sniffed the air twice, his long nasal hairs flapping with each short inhalation. His eyes scanned the crowd for a perpetrator. BAM. He spotted a superfan. It really wasn't that hard. The guy had a terrible beard, big glasses, and a Styx t-shirt peeking out from under his burnt orange, polyester tux jacket. Craig made a beeline through the crowd and quietly but sternly questioned the man. I wonder how those guys even found out about the Styx concert, let alone got into the hotel. Maybe there was some sort of a classic rock signal that flashed in the sky like Batman. Maybe there was an underground classic rock society that met in caves and drank Coors Light from cans wrapped in neon koozies. Perhaps they whipped their long hair around while they showed off their guitar picks they caught at that super rad concert they went to back in '92. Maybe these things exist. I'd like to hope so.

Soon all the party crashers were cleared out, dinner was served, dessert came and went, and the crowd was abuzz with excited chatter about their pending rock and roll adventure. If I listened closely I could hear "back in the day" stories about previous Styx experiences, teenage drunken vomit stories, or how their room used to be covered in Styx posters.

Then it happened.

The lights went out. The stage lit up. The women, with their high heels and silicone chests, jumped out of their chairs

---

[24] Most important side note in this whole book so listen up you little twerps: I Googled Zubaz on a whim, and I came across… the Zubaz website. Oh yes, they have a website, and yes, you can still buy them in a wide variety of neon colors and zebra patterns. Long live the Zubaz.

and began screaming like they were sixteen again. Styx emerged. It looked like they had never even entered the 21st century. Their hair was still long and flowing in the wind, leather still plastered to their bodies, and their mustaches still making onlookers uncomfortable. Ew mustaches. Shave them old men, shave them young hipsters, everyone just shave them.

As the Palm Beachers engrossed themselves into the concert whilst daydreaming about the night they first kissed Tommy in the back of his black Trans-am Firebird, I too found my mind wandering back to a time before Barack Obama and Skype. I too dreamed of what it would have been like to have Styx be my first concert experience, mid 1980's style. My hair would have been bigger than a Texans and freshly permed, of course. I would have worn my favorite black Styx T-shirt and cut-off jeans. I imagined I would have gone with a boy named Billy or Zane, and perhaps would have made out in the back of his Delorean after the show, our breath tart from the fruit punch wine coolers. Why did I have to spend my teenage years in such a non-tacky decade? What did the early 2000's give us? Episodes of Friends and Nokia cell phones? Boring.

Styx played an amazing concert. It was quite entertaining to see the men rocking it out like they never went out of style. They oozed cool, they actually looked okay in a mullet, and their moustaches were not too disenchanting. I was sold, and will now forever be a Styx fan.

Soon after the show wrapped up, Craig cornered me and ordered me to go pick up the hotel's boardroom. Buzz kill. I trudged down the hall to my cleaning doom. The boardroom is a long, narrow, drenched in tacky wallpaper and overpowered by a massive conference table that fifteen people could sleep on top of comfortably, if such an occasion ever arose. It is good to think about things like this. You never know what can happen in this day and age.

When I walked in, I quietly cursed. The room was completely trashed. Half eaten sandwiches, tipped over bottles of soda, and dozens of nasty crumpled napkins containing God knows what lay everywhere. I began shuffling through the mess, and came across something we don't usually serve at the hotel -- an array of organic throat-coating tea. And wait a second, was that a crushed up can of Tab soda I see? Who would require such specific, odd beverage choices? I gasped. I was in the dressing room of Styx, my new favorite band that I would probably never listen to again. I was in awe.

I put my celebrity shock aside, and continued my clean up. The food was hardly touched: a couple of chicken salad sandwiches were half eaten and a few Cokes had been sipped on. A few of the throat-coat tea bags had been opened and steeped, and it made my laugh. I could just imagine them after a crazy show, going back, putting their bifocals back on, wrapping up in a comfy robe and sipping tea, organic tea at that, in front of a fire. Oh, to be a middle-aged rock star.

As I continued to clean, I found some price tags from their clothing they had ripped off before the show. I couldn't help but check out how much it costs to look as fab as Styx. One T-shirt - size small - was over one hundred bucks! Who knew it cost so much to look so grungy?

I threw out the tags and started clearing off the massive table. There were some papers and crumpled napkins, but then, at the end of the table, I spotted something very strange. It was a massive pile of Band-Aids.

Used Band-Aids. This is where I draw my waitressing line. Listen up Styx, listen real close. I don't care how much I enjoyed your rocking display of musical excellence, I did not enjoy cleaning up a massive pile of used wound covering adhesives that you left on top of the table. Perhaps next time you can throw them in the trash. Thank you. Rock on. Gross.

Plastic Chairs + Obese America = Bad Idea

I walked into the ballroom and the first thing I noticed was that the rented chairs for the evening were made out of flimsy, clear plastic. If you squinted you may not even know there were chairs at all. How couture. I walked over to one of the glorified lawn chairs and took a seat to test it out. It creaked and wiggled under my weight, and I felt it could collapse at any moment. I am just a small lass in a tuxedo, and if I felt uneasy sitting in the Barbie playhouse chair, I was sure it was not going to do so well under the weight of big, burly American men. Just as I was thinking this, I heard someone to the right of me, apparently having the same thought. A huge man, weighing at least 300 pounds, had arrived at the function early to scope out the room. He was wringing his hands, sweat forming on his brow as he assessed the flimsy chair situation.

He glanced at me and we locked eyes, his full of nervousness and embarrassment. "Ah, miss," he said. "I don't think these chairs are going to hold me. Do you have anything else?"

"Oh, of course!" I said in my best five star, I get paid to give you anything you want waitress voice, and I rushed to get him one of the sturdy chairs that usually come standard in the ballroom. When I returned, we discretely swapped it for a plastic fork chair at one of the tables in the back. He sat down on the new, well-built, metal and cloth chair, and smiled with a sigh of relief.

"Thanks. I've been known to break a few normal chairs in my day, and I know that those wouldn't hold me."

"Oh, of course, sir!" I cheerfully replied, still using that same, slightly higher than normal, helpful waitress tone of voice. Where does that come from anyway? Why does my voice go up an octave when I am trying to be hospitable? But the truth is, I was happy to give him a new, sturdy place to sit. The man was funny, kind, and looked me in the eye and talked to me as if I were actually a human being. We exchanged names, I told him to have a great evening and actually meant it, and walked back to the kitchen to begin pre-party preparations.

After about fifteen minutes, the crowd began to pour in. I was standing by my table, and before I could even lap napkins for my guests I was already being bombarded with special requests for the evening. "Ah, excuse me?" A man barked. I hustled over to him, almost tripping over my ugly black loafers.

"Yes, sir?"

"Can I get a Miller Light, please?" he spat out, not a hint of a smile on his face.

"Oh, I am sorry, sir. Budweiser is sponsoring tonight's event. I can get you a Bud Light if you would like." This was the truth: we only were allowed to offer Budweiser products that evening, bosses' order.

He looked at me, his square jaw tense, and said, "Get me a Miller Light." I stared at him and blinked twice. "Ah... Okay." What else was I supposed to say? He left no room for argument. So I went down to the basement beverage office to get the man a Miller Light. What a creep.

When I returned to the table I was again bombarded with annoying requests. "I'm vegan!" "Is your chicken free range? I only eat free range grain fed organic meats." "Can I have steamed veggies with no butter, no salt, no herbs and with carrots separated to the side." "NO DESSERT. If you set a dessert in front of me I am going to be very upset, so NO DESSERT."

Eventually I just ended up staring at these demanding people, forcing a smile, and trudging into the back to try and sort through all the requests. It wasn't even ten minutes into the event and it was already very evident that this group was going to be much more high maintenance than most.

There was a stage set up in the middle of the room, illuminated by an overhead cluster of spotlights, where a classical guitarist named Javier was going to croon the crowd for the evening. Javier had long, black, greased hair falling in waves around his perfectly tan face, his white veneers gleaming in the light. He looked like he should be a shirtless character on the cover of some terrible Spanish romance novel.

After spending twenty minutes in the back making sure everyone at my tables bizarre needs were taken care of, I reemerged into the ballroom and saw Javier was doing a weird hip thrust move on stage. Terrible. I avoided looking at the Latin sensation going all Ricky Martin on us, and began to set down the first course, a delicious and fattening, flaky, creamy mushroom strudel. One slice of strudel is a serving for the dignified guests, but in the back I could easily shove four down my throat, and then regret it the next day when the scale tells me I have gained five pounds of mushroomy fat and ungodly amounts of delicious sodium.

Once all my guests had their plates, I wandered back to the kitchen to avoid Javier's obnoxious guitar plucks and Spanish mutterings. I hadn't made it three steps when a man with a huge comb over snapped his fingers in my direction and threw out an, "Excuse me!"

I sighed, a little louder than I should have.

"Yes, sir, what can I do for you?" I winced as I said the words.

"What is this?" He was referring to his plate of steaming mushroom deliciousness.

"Mushroom strudel!" I replied, salivating at the thought of having one of my own later that evening.

"Is there mushrooms in it?"

Did he really just ask me that? I gotta get a new job.

"Ah, yes sir, there are mushrooms… in the mushroom strudel," I replied, trying with every ounce of my being not to sound sarcastic.

"What kind?"

Busted. I had no idea how to answer this question. Perhaps if I was super waitress I would have read my menu a little closer, or even faked an answer, but I just didn't care that much. However, I have been trained how to answer a question I do not know the answer to. Simple solution: just go and ask.

"I'm not sure, sir. If you would like I can go in the back and ask the ch-"

"NO!" he yelled, not even letting me finish my sentence. People near us had discreetly raised their eyes to watch the commotion. "How can you serve something if you don't know what it is? What if I have an allergy? This is absolutely unacceptable. Bring me a plain salad, oil and vinegar on the side! Do you think you could handle that?" His face was an ugly shade of red.

He shoved the strudel at my chest and I was speechless, in awe at the man's rudeness. I went in the back to annoy the chefs by asking for the plain salad. Ten minutes later, after they sent someone all the way down to the basement to assemble it, I brought it out to him. By then he was too wrapped up in conversation and fake laughter to even thank me. He took one bite of it and continued with his loud stories and booming laughter, then shoved it aside.

Sigh.

Soon it was time for the second course to be served, filet mignon as always, with a side of overly priced macaroni and cheese served in a mini skillet pan, and three asparagus spears on the side. Just three. The less you put on the plate, the more fancy it appears. I plopped the steak in front of Mr. Salad; he looked up at me, and I knew it was going to be round two.

"Um, is this filet mignon?"

"Yes, sir."

"How is it cooked?"

"Medium, sir."

"What is this sauce?" He continued his interrogation.

"Cabernet demi glace." I made sure to study the menu before I brought anything else out to this quizmaster.

"I only eat rare red meat, it has to be very red in the middle and I don't like cabernet demi –"

SHABOOM.

In the middle of his rant about the slab of beef, the plastic, flimsy chair below him flattened. His butt, shelled in his perfectly tailored pants, hit the floor. The plate of "overly cooked" filet he was holding in his hands had dumped all over his navy blue suit coat. He was flat on his back, his feet, clad in Italian leather loafers and no socks, sticking straight up in the air. The man was down and out, and covered in food.

I tried my best not to burst out laughing, and instead plucked the steak off of his chest and tried to help him up. Craig came running over with a wad of napkins and a sturdy chair, similar to the one I had provided for the nice round man before the party. Craig began his string of five star quality apologies.

The man was fuming. If he had gotten mad over mushrooms, you can only imagine how he reacted to being publically humiliated, injured, and covered in a sauce he didn't even want to eat in the first place. I did the best thing possible in that situation: I got out of there as fast as my little feet would take me. Even as I pushed through the heavy kitchen doors, I could still hear his yells over Javier's croons.

I looked down at the filet that I had pulled off of Mr. Rude's chest. I took a bite of it. Delicious. Don't judge me; I was on a nine-hour shift with no break.

As the party continued, three more chairs around the ballroom collapsed, and three more sturdy chairs and apologies were provided in exchange. When the night was over, the large, jolly man I had helped before the event found me in the hallway, and thanked me again for giving him a new chair. While everyone else was pulling a London Bridge and falling down, that man sat strong and confident all night. He slipped me a $20 tip to further express his appreciation.

Just as I was saying thank you, Mr. Huff and Puff walked by us; his shirt was stained by the cabernet demi-glace he so despised and there was a macaroni noodle in his hair. I smiled and gave him an artificial "Have a great evening," and he growled and mumbled something in grouch language. Who knew plastic chairs were also capable of doling out justice? WHO KNEW.

Flying Bride

Hava nagila
Hava nagila
Hava nagila vi nis'mecha

Hava neranenah
Hava neranenah
Hava neranenah vi nis'mecha

Uru, uru achim!
Uru achim b'lev sameach

Uru achim, uru achim!
B'lev sameach

To some that may sound like Ewok language, but to me that is the sound of a good time. Palm Beach has a very large Jewish population, and the majority of the weddings celebrated at the hotel follow Jewish tradition. That song, Hava Nagila, kicks off the reception and leads into a night of pure bliss. Every guest piles onto the tiny dance floor, makes a circle and starts dancing around and around until joy is bursting out of every one of their pores. The dance floor is more hopping than a club in Daytona Beach during spring break. Trust me, I know. I don't want to talk about it.

The best part of this traditional dance is when the bride and the groom are lifted up into the air, each grabbing a corner of a napkin, and are twirled and whirled around. I envy these brides. This looks like one of the most exhilarating and joyous moments of their life. The most exciting dance at my wedding was when they played 'Get Low' by Lil John and my grandma got down and dirty, almost breaking a hip in the process.

Jewish weddings are absolutely amazing, rich in tradition and celebration. I was setting up for the evening and quickly noticed a chuppah in the ceremony room, so I knew this one was going to be a winner.

The ceremony came and went, the glass was broken, and the bride and groom emerged into the ballroom to make sure every detail was in order for their looming celebration. I had been finishing up some tasks around the reception room and now was standing at attention with a tray of champagne, so this was the first time I saw the happy couple. The bride looked absolutely beautiful: her hair was swept back, and she had antique earrings dangling from her ears. She had bleached blonde hair, a perfect tan… and she must have weighed 400 pounds. Now, I have absolutely nothing against women who have a little more to love, God bless them, but as soon as I saw her, I thought of that chair dance looming in her very near future.

What was going to happen? The dance is absolutely necessary to complete the Jewish festivities, and the world would probably explode if it were skipped.

I glanced at the bride and noticed she was looking nervously at the two chairs that were already placed near the edge of the dance floor. I saw her face go white, and she was wringing her hands. Clearly, she too was thinking about the airborne dance that was quickly approaching. She made a bee line to the bar and gulped down a glass of champagne in one swig, then ordered another. Her new husband quietly tried to protest, but she would not hear it. She was knocking those things back like they were cheap shots of tequila. She took a deep breath and one more glass of bubbly for the road before the guests began pouring in, and plastered a big, fake smile on her face to greet them.

Hors d'oeuvres were passed, wine was sipped, and laughter filled the air. I kept one eye on the bride as we quickly approached her fated moment. She rushed to the bar just as the music began playing, and quickly took a shot of whisky.

Hava nagila

Hava nagila

Hava nagila vi nis'mecha

The bride's face dropped, just as everyone else's lifted. The clapping and cheering began, and the dance floor filled. The crowd pushed the couple out in front of the stage, their chairs awaiting them. The groom carelessly plopped down on his as the bride hesitantly sat on hers, her nervousness still masked behind her pretty, fake smile. Every groomsman in the wedding party surrounded her. The groom must have played college football: all of his friends had necks bigger than Brett Favre's, with muscles definition visible even through their tight tuxedo sleeves. It almost seemed as if the groom had selected his strongest, beefiest friends to be his groomsmen, knowing that this bride-lifting moment was to come. I held my breath. I felt as if I was watching a suspenseful movie, and suddenly had a strong urge for popcorn.

The guests were spinning around and around, the music getting louder and louder. The groomsmen counted - "one...two...THREE" - and heaved the large bride into the air. A drunken smile burst across her face as she realized she was up. She locked eyes with her groom and reached for her end of the napkin. But just then, it all came loose. A meathead groomsman tripped over a renegade high heel on the edge of the dance floor and lost his balance.

The entire group of men supporting the bride started to sway. Her face dropped, as did her hand from the napkin. The reality of the situation settled over her. She knew, I knew, we all knew what was about to happen. They swayed left, they swayed right. Some brave, optimistic soul tried to stand below the woman in an attempt to catch her, but we all knew it was useless; he would just be squished. Possibly to death. The bride was going down, and was taking everyone in a five-foot radius with her.

Her arms flailed as she tried to grab onto the chair, onto her groom, anything! But at this point, nothing would help except for a massive safety net, which, unfortunately, is not included in our wedding packages. She tipped forward, off the chair, her arms and legs flailing. The crowd below her could not support her booty-licious body, and she and the eight groomsmen beneath her were flattened.

The *Hava Nagila* slowly came to a stop. There was four seconds of extremely awkward, torturous silence. Then, in unison, everyone gasped and started buzzing around, trying to help the bride up, call a doctor, anything to try and ease the tension. But then, a wedding miracle. The bride pushed away all those trying to assist her and scurried to her feet. A little blood was trickling down her forehead.

All the guests held their breath, waiting to see if she would cry, yell or pass out. But instead, a huge smile broke out across her face, and she yelled "woo hoo!" Her arms pumped the air in victory. Her joyous exclamation was a little slurred. It seemed as if the excessive champagne self-medication had done its job. She felt no pain from her fall, nor any embarrassment. Oh champagne, the salve of all terrible wedding moments. With that the band started up again, and the festivities continued for one of the liveliest wedding receptions I have ever witnessed.

The next morning I was scheduled to work the post-wedding brunch. The bride walked in, her hand tightly clasped with that of her glowing groom, her wedding ring gleaming in the morning sunlight. They were smiling, laughing, and greeting all their guests. But if the light hit her just right, I could see under her freshly powdered face that the bride had a black eye and a Band-Aid peeked out from under the knee length hem of her dress. Despite those injuries, she looked radiant as she gazed lovingly at her new husband, winking at him over the top of the glass of her third mimosa.

Cream, Sugar or Pee?

You know when you are at a party and there is always "that guy?" His name is Matt, or Brian, or Zak with a K. Something from the 80's and mundane. His tie is dedicated to his favorite college sports team, and is most likely a clip on. His face is red and sweaty from all the alcohol pumping through his cheeseburger-clogged veins. He talks so loudly and so close to your ear that your eardrums buzz afterwards like you've just attended a KISS concert and sat next to the speakers. But the most defining characteristic of "that guy" is that you are ninety-six percent sure that at any moment he is about to upchuck the twenty-four Bud Lights he has downed in the past two hours.

Well, "that guy" was present at one particular event. It was a wedding, of course. Weddings are about the only time where ex-college frat boys show up at the hotel, and, with the help of the open bar, create complete chaos. Matt, Brian, Zak with a K – whatever, was at this party in all his glory.

Early in the reception I noticed him, as he kept wandering past my tables to the open bar; each trip his steps became more stumbled, his voice became louder and more slurred. The light reflected off his overly gelled hair, and his face was red as a vine-ripened tomato. Somewhere between the fourteenth or and fifteenth trip back to the bar, Matt-Brian-Zak with a K heard a tune that struck his fancy, and he meandered his way to the dance floor and whipped out the ultimate worst dance move of all time– the worm. Oh the worm, how I loath you. Perhaps at the seventh grade dance when we were first introduced I enjoyed your silliness and felt slightly impressed by your complicated movements. But now, forty-nine parties later, it is far past the time of your retirement. When this parties "that guy" decided to flop back and forth on the dance floor atop his round, beer-filled belly, I cringed. But he did it, proud and strong. At one point he tipped a little too far forward and smacked his face on the granite floor, but this did not stop his epic dance moment. He flailed around like a dead fish for a solid two minutes, until finally the DJ changed the track and the worming stopped. The entire ballroom breathed a sigh of relief.

As Matt-Brian-Zak with a K brushed the dust off his navy blue suit coat, he made his way back to the bar for another drink, which he promptly chugged. Apparently all those hot dance moves really build up a thirst. Seven beers later, after all the courses had been served and coffee was being passed, Matt-Brian-Zak with a K strolled his way out of the ballroom and down the hallway. Perhaps he was about to "break the seal," a party term my New Jersey friends taught me. Oh New Jersey, I can always count on you for the proper party lingo.

Fifteen minutes went by and the party boy was nowhere to be found. Perhaps he fell asleep in the elevator, or fell off the sea wall into the ocean? I hoped not the latter. Most of my guests had left by now, so I wandered into the back with a tray of dirty dishes and a need for a Diet Coke. The kitchen was empty, except for a cluster of dirty glasses that needed to be taken down to the basement. I was about to enter the cooler to satisfy my craving for artificial sweeteners and caffeine when I heard a rustle from the small back corner room where we store the coffee pots. My mind immediately thought – ghost. As an avid watcher of Ghost Hunters on the SyFy Channel, I have always been disappointed by the lack of supernatural activity that goes on in this massive, extremely old hotel. I mean come on, not even one ghost story? I guess all the spirits are as freaked out by the socialites as I am.

Putting on my bravery tuxedo, I headed back into the room to investigate the mystery noise. Was it a fellow server indulging in a leftover dinner? Was it a massive jungle rat that made his way inside through the air vent? No, it was neither. There, surrounded by the shelves of coffee pots, sat "that guy."

The worm-dancing, drunk ex-frat boy had passed out in our back room, a beer glass still resting in his hand. "Ah, sir?" I called out gently. No response.

"Sir?" I said again as I began to shake his shoulder. He awakened, looked around, confused, and then eventually focused on my face.

"Hey…" He paused here and belched. "Baby," he muttered. His breath reeked of cigarette smoke. I shuddered.

"Sir, you are in our coffee pot room. You can't be in here," I told him. He began laughing at me as if I had just told the best joke of all time.

"Haha, so funny, but seriously, you need to get out of here before my supervisor finds you and calls security," I said. That seemed to sober him up one fraction of a percent, just enough for him to work his way up to his feet. I guided him to the elevator, asked him what floor and pressed three as he instructed, and wished him a good night as the elevator doors closed. I hoped he at least made it out of the elevator before passing out again.

I returned to the kitchen, downed that Diet Coke, and went back into the ballroom to finish cleaning up before Craig let us all go home. I went straight to bed, exhausted from my shift and not looking forward to the next one, which started in approximately six hours. I was working breakfast, always an easy shift, except for the ungodly hour I have to get my butt out of bed.

The next morning, I woke to Florida sunshine and parrots screeching outside my bedroom window. Yes, we actually do have a flock of parrots that fly around the West Palm Beach and Palm Beach area. They are small, green, and extremely loud, but still cute. They actually have created a nest at the hotel, and every night around sunset they make their way to the ocean lawn where they roost, screeching at the top of their little bird lungs. Conveniently, their nest is perched right next to where the outdoor wedding ceremonies are held. The parrots always manage to arrive just as couples are saying their vows against a sunset-filled sky. Their squawking is extremely distracting, and to me, hilarious. When planning their wedding, guests probably don't think of it being crashed by a flock of parrots, but hey, at least it makes a good story.

Kyle and I drove our Toyota into the employee parking lot, our tuxedos smelling a little funky from last night's event. We run into Craig just as we were clocking in.

"You two! Wake up, you happy couple, and go upstairs and get the coffee ready," he ordered, his voice reminding me of the flock of parrots. We trudged upstairs to the kitchen and back into the coffee pot room, where Mr. Drunk Face had passed out the night before. The pots were still festively disheveled from where he had collapsed. Kyle and I straightened them out a bit, and picked up a couple pots to take over to the coffee station to be filed.

"Hey," Kyle said, his face quizzical as he was scrambling to hold all of his coffee pots with one arm. "This pot still has coffee in it, I think. I hate when people don't empty them," he grumbled.

We walked over to the coffee station and set the pots down. He took the one with the liquid in it over to the sink to rinse it out as I began filling up a clean carafe.

"Oh, oh my gosh, SICK," I heard Kyle yell, followed by a clang as he dropped the pot into the stainless steel sink.

"What? Moldy coffee?" I asked, but not really caring because it was still far too early to actually have feelings.

"Get over here, this is sick. Oh man, I'm going to puke." Now I was intrigued. I walked over and opened the lid to the coffee pot, which had landed upright. Instead of black, cold coffee as I expected, the pot was half filled with a dark yellow, salty-smelling liquid.

Pee. Freaking pee.

SICK.

I gagged and drew my hand back, knocking over the pot. The sticky liquid spilled out, and a bit splashed up onto my jacket.

"That freaking drunk guy!" I yelled. Kyle looked confused. "I found him in there last night, he must have peed in that pot before passing out. This is unbelievable."

Kyle, being the brave, amazing husband he is (he is the one that always kills renegade cockroaches in our apartment) wrapped his hand in paper towels like cotton candy and picked up the heavy, silver pot. He chucked it into the recycling, and covered it up with the towels so nobody spotted it and thought it got thrown out by mistake. I don't care if that pot was made out of solid diamonds, it must NEVER be used again. Never.

Kyle and I each washed our hands fifty times, with the same precision I have learned from watching Grey's Anatomy. I doused them with so much anti-bacterial gel that my hands stung. The remainder of my shift felt disgusting. I felt dirty. Although I scrubbed and scrubbed the tiny fleck of urine that made it onto my jacket, I still felt like every time I walked fast a wave of pee smell made it to my nose.

I didn't see the drunk guy that morning. I am sure he was either sleeping off a huge hangover, or had already checked out of the hotel. If I did see him, I would have offered him a cup of coffee, and asked if he would like cream, sugar, or pee with it. Judging from his level of inebriation, I am sure he would not even recognize me, nor remember peeing in a coffee pot in the heart of one of the classiest hotels in the world. But I would have loved to remind him.

500 Chopsticks and Two Bush Sisters

South Florida summer heat makes me want to take all my clothes off, run through the streets with a BB gun and shoot the lizards as they try and scurry from my path. I hate the summer heat. I just had to get that off my chest. Moving on.

One night, I worked a rehearsal dinner for a huge wedding. Our boss has been talking about this wedding for over a year, so basically we had put on our best pair of K-mart grandma loafers; it was time to bring the big guns. I looked at the rundown for the evening: dinner from 7:00 to 9:00, first course, a beet and goat cheese salad, then short ribs, and fruit sundaes for dessert. Beets taste like dirt and short ribs creep me out, so I was not very excited about the next couple of hours. But just as I was planning a devious scheme to steal sushi from the neighboring party, I noticed something very peculiar at the bottom of the paper. It read "VVVIP."

Okay, so either someone had a hand cramp and didn't click spell check, or this was a triple VIP event. VVVIP. I wondered what I would have to do in my life to surpass the status of VIP and move to VVVIP. At this point, if I ever even got an IP I would feel accomplished.

So there were three V's and 300 people heading our way. I went into our main ballroom to rally up some silverware. A lovely little Turkish co-worker came up to me and whispered in her broken English, "Bush daughter, Barbara. Right there in big poof blue dress." What? Was this little adorable Turkey bundle of joy trying to tell me that Barbara Bush was in our midst? Indeed, she was.

I zeroed in on who I *thought* Barbara Bush was; however, it turned out someone else decided to don a blue poufy dress as well, so for ten minutes I was eyeballing another chick with brown hair who I suspected used to roam the White House. Nope, not Barbara. As an aspiring journalist one would think that I would be familiar with the former president's daughter, but I wasn't. Nobody really was, actually. While I do think I could pick Chelsea Clinton out of a crowd based on her afro poof perm hair, Barbara Bush Jr. has just somehow slipped through my radar.

Eventually, I got my brown-haired, blue-clothed women straightened out, and there she was in all her glory. President Bush's daughter. Fascinating. Since I had had no luck stealing sushi rolls yet, staring at Barbara Bush was so far the most exciting part of my evening.

A particularly liberal server friend of mine, Karl, was all a fluster over the sight of Bush blood within his midst. Karl, who enjoys participating in puppy store protests and has more bumper stickers on the back of his Prius than I had zits on my seventh grade face, told me that after he dropped Barbara's plate of ribs down in front of her, he was going to whisper "John Kerry" in her ear, then casually offer her sauce for her ribs. "You won't," I dared him. He didn't. The night pressed on and the small wedding rehearsal dinner blossomed into a large beach party. I was assigned to pass hors d'oeuvres, and I had my plate stacked with chocolate-dipped key lime pie on a stick. Each pie slice feels like it weighs about six pounds, and those six pounds go straight onto my left butt cheek after eating it. Try as I may to refrain from indulging in that lime-flavored lard on a stick, I ate one - okay, two- then immediately regretted it. But those seventeen seconds of shoving decadent sugary goodness down my throat were the best seventeen seconds of my entire eight-hour shift.

As the party expanded, so did the Bush family. Cue: Jenna Bush, keeping it classy with her DUI charge and Today Show career. As an aspiring journalist I do envy her cuddle sessions with Al Roker, but then again I am trying to launch my reporting career while graduating from a college nobody has ever heard of, while she launched hers from the White House. No big deal, it's just the White House. It's okay – I am not that upset. Al Roker is quite terrifying anyway, especially if you have not had any coffee before watching him.

Jenna stood in the center of a small crowd, wearing a white dress and tall heels, and there I was with my plate of pie, in my baggy tuxedo that had steak sauce stains down the front. I was staring at her impeccable blonde highlights when she whipped around and yelled, "Hey!" I looked over my polyester-covered shoulders. Nobody was behind me but a man with his head down on a table from drinking too much whisky. It appeared she was 'heying' at me.

"Ah, yes?"

"Do you want to play golf with this guy tomorrow?" She pointed behind her.

I followed her gesture. There stood a lanky, curly-haired man with a big Adam's apple, looking as confused as I was. In true five star quality serving fashion I answered, with excitement in my voice that I didn't actually feel, "Sure! Of course I will play golf with you," just to appease their weird party conversation. The tall man shrugged, and I stood there, confused. Her off beat question didn't throw me too far off, as I am quite used to being asked bizarre things from random guests who either had too much to drink, or too much money to keep them in touch with reality. And besides, as my mother always says, consider the source. She is a Bush, nobody can ever understand what they are talking about.

With that, Jenna whipped her head back around to the band of followers surrounding her and kept chattering away, seemingly unaware of the question she even asked me. So how do I, the slickest, coolest waitress of all time, handle that uncomfortable situation? I stuck my tray in the middle of their circle and offered up my key lime pie on a stick.

Cricket.

I received no response from anybody. Not even a "no thank you," just one big ignore session. Awesome.

I walked back to the kitchen with my pie plate still full. When I got inside, Craig looked at me with that 'look' in his eye, the same look I have seen in terrorists on the news and Martha Stewart when her co-host messes up on their craft project. A look of pure, unadulterated evil.

"Craig, what do you want?" I asked, not wanting to know the answer.

His lip quivered a little before he barked out "You," pointing at me. He kept his arm extended and swung it around 180 degrees to point at Kristin. "And you. Go downstairs. Now." So Kristin and I trudged our way down to the employee basement, confused at Craig's actions and yet curious at the same time. Perhaps we would be getting out early? Perhaps we would be sent to clean up a buffet, aka shove as much of it down our throats as possible before throwing it in the trash. Perhaps this was yet again another time where I am too optimistic for my own good.

When we got into the banquet office, we saw a huge pile of chopsticks sitting in the middle of the room. My eyes immediately scanned the room for renegade plates of sushi, but none were to be found. A manager named Albert, who has an ungodly large mustache and who usually only speaks to us servers if we are getting written up or fired, poked his head out of his corner cubicle. "Hey. We need you to peel the labels off of every single pair of these chopsticks, then you can go home."

Excuse me? Was this going to be an early out, or a life sentence of peeling off labels? Only time would tell. At that point I was just grateful I was going to be able to sit down, which is a rare treat in the waitressing world.

I picked up a pair of the chopsticks. They were black and plastic, with a red sticker wrapped around their center to keep them together. I held my breath and tried to remove it, hoping it would come off with a simple tug. About one fraction of a centimeter peeled off, leaving a mass of sticky residue and paper plastered on. This was when the reality of my chopstick fate set in. This was going to take all night.

In my slightly spoiled and overly outspoken fashion, I

pleaded with everyone in the office, trying to convince them this job was completely unnecessary and absolutely ridiculous. I mean, the red label looks great, right? In my desperation to not spend the next fifteen hours scraping sticker residue off of plastic sticks, I even approached the massive mustache man. He just looked at me and said, "It's not even worth trying." He left us with our massive pile of stickered chopsticks and misery while he called it a night and drove his Mercedes home.

Kristin and I had no choice now but to suck it up and settle in for a long, intimate relationship with ugly plastic sushi eating utensils. Fifteen minutes went by, forty minutes, *one hour*.

The rest of the servers finished cleaning up the party upstairs and came down into the office. I let out a sigh of relief. All right, teamwork time! We could knock out this stupidly tedious job in ten more minutes, easy. My co-workers looked at our fingers, nearly raw from trying to peel off hundreds of the tiny stickers, shook their heads, and made up every excuse possible to get out of that office and leave us to our fate. "I work breakfast in the morning." "I'm on a double shift." I have arthritis," (said the one eighty year old server). "I'm allergic to fish." (I don't know how that one makes any sense.) What they really meant was, "What you are doing looks like it sucks, and I can't muster up the kindness in my heart to help you out." Thanks, tuxedo pals, thanks for nothing.

DFKJDHFJHDKFJD. This was the sound of my frustration at this point. *Another hour* went by, and we had about ten boxes left. Craig burst into the room. "You're not done yet?" he exclaimed in his thick accent. I almost jabbed a chopstick into his right eye, but refrained because I didn't want to clean up the blood.

Craig picked up a set of the sticks, and began trying to peel the wrapper off with his pudgy fingers. "What! This is ca-ca!" I don't know why an Indian uses the Spanish word ca-ca, but he does. I will never understand anything about this man. But indeed, it truly was ca-ca; that is what we were trying to explain two hours and 480 chopstick sets ago. "All right, go home," Craig said. Those were the most beautiful words I had heard since my wedding vows. I literally just completed the most pointless job of all time. My dark purple manicured nails were chipped, and my thumbs were cramping in ways I never thought possible. But I was released, and at that point it was all I cared about. My loafers somehow led me to my car, exhausted after a long night of Jenna Bush and chopsticks. Whoever ate with those plastic sushi devices had better appreciate them and their sticker-free glory. They won't.

Your Engagement Ring Smells Like Whisky

I was standing outside of a bustling party, watching a coat rack with a single coat on it. I had been there for an hour. Let's discuss this scenario. First of all, we are in South Florida, practically in Cuba, for that matter. Why do we have a coat rack? Second of all, was I really getting paid for this? Let me check … yes, I was. The owner of that single coat was inside the ballroom, attending the most excessive birthday party of all time. The room was decorated floor to ceiling in sparkling rhinestone-covered fabric. There were fifteen disco balls spinning over the dance floor, and there were two huge elephants on either side made completely out of hot pink roses. It was amazing, it was glorious, it was breathtaking, and it was all for some thirty-two year old's birthday. It wasn't even a significant birthday like forty of fifty, just… thirty-two. I could only imagine what her birthday was like when she turned twenty-one.

I was standing there with my new friend the fur coat (where was PETA when you *actually* needed them?), quietly tapping my black, tube sock-covered toes to the beat of the band, when the heavy wooden ballroom doors came flying open, making a loud crash as they slammed into the wall, the noise startling in the empty, cold hallway. A man stumbled out and nearly did a face plant. He caught his balance by grabbing onto the coat rack, and somehow managed to focus his eyes on mine. It only took me about two seconds to realize that man was more drunk than my Aunt Lisa on Christmas right after her poodle

Fofo died. RIP Fofo, eating two pounds of sour skittles is a tragic way to go, but also a delicious way.

His red glassy eyes squinted at me. "Which way ..." he slurred, and paused for a few seconds to catch his breath and let out an extremely stinky burp, before continuing "... to the ocean?"

"East," I replied.

"Huh?" he spit out, his face contorted in confusion. Obviously, someone wasn't a boy scout growing up.

"It's this way, sir," I replied, and gestured with my hand toward the mighty Atlantic. The man wobbled his way back into the party, using the wall to hold himself up. I heard him yell, "Tina!" and instantly had flashbacks of "Napoleon Dynamite." However, instead of a sleepy llama emerging from the party, out walked a blonde with high heels so tall they would make a midget look of average height. Drunk Master Funk leaned all of his weight on Tina the Blonde and they began walking outside, slowly and carefully, as the man swerved around like a bumble bee in flight.

That man is two steps away from hurling, I thought to myself, and assumed that was why he was making the trek outside. I looked around for Craig, a janitor, or anyone else besides me that could take care of the vomit catastrophe that was about to erupt. I don't do puke clean ups. I think cleaning pee out of a coffee pot already qualifies me as server of the year, thank you very much.

There was not a single soul in sight except for an ancient socialite wearing big, obnoxious, black-rimmed glasses, shuffling her way down the hallway. Old turtle eyes wasn't going to help the vomit man, and neither was I. He was on his own. I continued my job of standing and existing, staring at the single coat on the coat rack.

A few minutes later I was hit with a warm, salty breeze as the sliding glass doors opened up and Tina and Mr. Wastey Face stumbled back into the building. My eyes darted across his tuxedo, scanning for traces of puke. But instead of upchucked sushi, I saw something sparkly on Tina's left hand that wasn't there before. An engagement ring. Mr. Alcoholics Anonymous had stumbled, and boy do I mean stumbled, out to the ocean side to propose. Not exactly every girl's dream, that when the man dips to one knee he topples over and begins dry heaving. But, nonetheless, Tina looked happy - ecstatic, for that matter.

Drunk McGee stumbled over to me and shoved Tina's hand under my nose, her fingers smelling of whiskey and maraschino cherries. 'Look... burp... what I did!" he gargled, as he began slowly leaning forward towards me, past the point of acceptable personal space.

"Oh... it's beautiful. Congratulations!" I exclaimed, trying not to burst out laughing, and dodging to the side so the intoxicated man didn't topple over on me, as he was now leaning forward at about a forty-eight degree angle. Tina and Mr. Drunk Proposal started laughing, as Tina helped him to stand up straight, then the happy couple spent a good two minutes making out a mere three feet from me and my friend the fur coat. I began counting the fox hairs on it, in a desperate attempt to avert my eyes from the train wreck exchanging saliva next to me.

Finally they came up for air, just as the drunk man let out another burp, and the happy couple headed back into the ballroom. I stood there dumbfounded. Usually at a time like that, it would be customary to offer the couple a bottle of champagne, but I thought I probably shouldn't in that case. After another hour of coat watching, and three more slow passes from the old socialite with the ugly glasses, the owner of the fur coat returned for it and left, the party wrapped up, and Tina and Drunk Master Funk went home to begin their new life together. First step was probably taking some Advil and drinking a large glass of water.

Why Don't We Just Eat Cash and Call It A Night?

Listen up kids, listen up real close. By now you have probably come to realize that to host an event on Palm Beach, especially at the hotel, it costs a hefty chunk of change. You want to party like a big shot? You'd better have the wallet to back it up. But just how much does it cost to, say, hold your nuptials at our beautiful, historic ocean-side hotel? Well… a lot.

For example, one lovely bride to be had everything in order. She had the ring, she had the venue, and she had the dress. But in all the planning, one minor detail was overlooked - her relationship. A few months before the wedding, she stared at her future spouse and said – "hold up, I just remembered there is life after a wedding ceremony. Let's get real, I don't care how much money you have, I hate your terrible comb over, and I know you slept with your assistant last May. I can't go through with this – the wedding is off." Ouch.

However, with the wedding being called off so near to the date, there was no way to get her deposit back. How much had already been invested in the wedding that was non-refundable? One freaking million dollars, and no way to get it back. The space has been reserved, things have been ordered; there was just no way for that refund to happen.

So, what does the little ex-bride-to-be do? She took that million dollars and re-formatted the entire event. What was once a wedding for 300-plus guests was now condensed to a small gathering for a mere thirty of her closest friends and family. Oh, how nice, you may be thinking, what a great idea. But perhaps you mis-understand the magnitude of this small party. She had ONE MILLION DOLLARS to spend among thirty people.

It started with dinner. Now if I was to go out and, say, have a fancy, expensive dinner with my husband, I could not fathom spending more than about twenty-five dollars a person - I am just that poor and cheap. Working at the hotel, I have seen some pretty pricey dinner tabs. A 300-dollar dinner never ceases to amaze me, yet I serve them all the time. But in this case, 300 dollars is just chump change. The former bride had to go way above and beyond to reach her million dollar budget. The cost of ONE dinner per person was $1,400. Make it rain.

What on God's great earth can you put on a plate that costs over a grand per person? That was the part that blew my mind. I have served dinners starting from around $100 a plate to, now, $1,400. And they all look exactly the same. A hunk of filet mignon, a fan of asparagus or other vegetables, a delicious dollop of mashed potatoes, and you have yourself a dinner. That $1,400 dinner looked exactly like the $400 dinner I served last week. I didn't understand the difference. Maybe there was a magical elixir mixed into the sauce that removed all the guests' wrinkles and instantly filled their wallets with a stack of hundred dollar bills, I don't know. But what I do know is that if I was going to spend over one grand on one dinner, I would want it to have magical powers, sing to me before I ate it, turn into solid gold upon digestion, and then... well, you know what I mean.

All I could think of was what else $1,400 could buy me. Well according to the all-wise oracle, I could buy a forest green 1992 Toyota Camry for about that same price. If the air conditioning works, that sounds good to me. Or I could buy an entire year's worth of delicious, overly priced caramel lattes at Starbucks, low fat milk please. I know I would be five points more happy if every single day started out with one of those delectable treats. $1,400 could also buy 466 bags of Doritos. Why Doritos, you ask? Because Doritos are freaking delicious. If I wanted to become obese, I would do so by eating Doritos. I dream about this sometimes. Sigh.

Anyway, the ex-bride to be did not serve up a junky car with a side of cool ranch Doritos, rather a classy five course meal. One would think that the main course was steak stuffed with purred dollar bills covered in a gold glace, but alas, it was just plain 'ole steak.

Side note- eating gold is actually something that goes on in these freaky parts of the world. My friend works at Mar-a-Lago, which is Donald Trump's house just a few miles from the hotel. She brought home cookies that had real gold painted on after her shift once. Sometimes in life you come across things you eat just to say that you ate it. That was one of those times. I ate the gold-covered cookie, and I felt like a ridiculous and spoiled American because of it. Please don't try eating your wedding band, it won't taste good, and I am sure it would be terrible to digest.

The Cristal was flowing freely, of course, at this money spending party. Bottle after bottle was popped and served. Okay, honesty time again, because I am terrible at keeping secrets. I snuck a sip of the Cristal in the back room. A tiny sip. Let's just say they don't serve bottles of champagne over $15 in Coon Rapids, Minnesota. Olive Garden is the most fancy restaurant around, for goodness sake. I did some math (a once a year event for me), and I figured my tiny sip of Cristal would probably cost around $20. No big deal, I just drank a trip to the movies.

The rest of the money must have been spent on decorations, the live music (which was pretty amazing), and the mystery gift bags that were handed out at the end of the evening. I didn't get to peek in one, but I could only imagine their contents. "Oh look, Charles, she bought us each a country in Africa, how thoughtful."

The whole evening amazed me. I am just a wee Midwesterner whose price per head at her wedding was a mere $25, not much more than the tiny sip of champagne I snuck in the dusty kitchen corridor. But you know what? Even though I didn't serve gold and expensive champagne, I did have a wicked cheese plate, two-buck-chuck drinks at the cash bar, an abundance of wonderful, priceless memories, and a brand new husband whom I adore. I say our parties were about equal.

Does Happiness Cost Extra?

I wish every story in here could be about perverted, creepy senators and cakes that cost as much as a small home in Nebraska, but the fact of the matter is sometimes life isn't as funny as one would hope. Wait, am I about to get all emo on you? Yes I am, minus the black swoopy haircut and band T-shirt.

It was late August, and stickier outside than the underside of a New York City subway railing. Shifts are scarce in these off-season days, so I was surprised when I got called into work. I traded in my yellow bandeau bikini for my beloved old friend the tuxedo, jumped in my Toyota and drove to work, stopping to get a coconut iced coffee from Dunkin Donuts on the way.

The main employee parking lot was full, a clear indicator that the night was going to be busy. I had to park way down the road in the overflow lot, a good seven-minute walk from the employee entrance, in the August heat, in a tuxedo. Not a good way to begin the night.

It was windy, so I had trouble opening the door to the dungeon basement where they hide all of us staff like little trolls. I defeated the sea breeze and made my way in, and was overcome with the delicious aroma that spilled out of the hotel bakery located just next to where we are to clock in. Fresh cookies always seem to be baking in the oven, and it is the first smell you encounter when starting your shift.

However, I only took one quick whiff because I knew as I rounded the corner I would be hit with the other smell that dominates the rest of the basement. The garbage room. Somebody had the terrible idea to place it right next to the heavenly-smelling bakery, as a cruel, cruel joke. A room that holds every disgusting thing every guest has disposed of, mixed with old food and death. It literally smells like rotten baby poop. I would put a scratch-n-sniff example in this book, but nobody would buy it or those actually brave enough to take a whiff would immediately fall ill. It is the absolute worst smell that has ever wafted under my little nose. What a good way to pump people up for work – starting their evening off with the stench of doom.

I checked the assignment board for the rundown on the night, and sure enough there was a massive party in our largest ballroom; around 400 people were to attend. It was a VIP function, so my serving skills would have to be at their best. Blah. Take me back to my piña colada sunbathing coma now, please.

I walked upstairs and was amazed at the sight. The room was completely transformed, unrecognizable. Flowers towered so high on every table, they almost touched the ceiling. The dance floor was lit up by hundreds of glass balls with candles burning inside of them, hanging by a clear string so it appeared they just floated in the air. The stage was huge and our best house band was already warming up for another night of keeping the party kicking.

Craig explained the crowd was going to be all locals. The party was somewhat of an end of the summer socialite soiree, to welcome people back from their summer spent in the Hamptons, or wherever they went to escape the sweltering Florida heat. No woman spared a penny on her outfit, and the men dressed in their Palm Beach finest, as well. This truly was the event of all events to be seen at.

The guests at my table all paid me little attention, in true Palm Beach fashion, being too caught up in summer gossip and flirtatious conversations. However, I noticed one man at my table had been quiet ever since the main course was served. As I went to clear his plate, I realized that his head was slumped down and his eyes were closed. Too much whisky, perhaps? But I looked closer and realized his lips were blue, and I immediately went into panic mode. I dropped his plate and ran to find Craig, my tuxedo tails flapping in the wind behind me as I darted across the crowded ballroom. We called 911 and it seemed the ambulance arrived in mere seconds. It didn't take long for fire rescue to respond on the island, it being only miles long and the only other time they see any action besides heart attacks and old ladies breaking a hip is when a renegade poodle gets its afro puff stuck in a tree branch and needs rescuing.

The EMTs put the man flat on his back, and removed his necktie and jacket. At that point, his face was starting to resemble Violet Beauregard from *Willy Wonka and The Chocolate Factory*. He was unconscious, and the whole ordeal was getting more frightening by the second. The band had stopped playing and a small crowd of about ten were standing nearby watching the drama unfold, while the rest of the party continued chatting, not seeming very interested in the chaos erupting.

The paramedics heaved the man onto the stretcher and ushered him out of the room, the heavy ballroom doors slamming behind them. Not knowing what to do with myself, I just went to clear the man's plate. Another guest who was sitting at the table grabbed my arm, looked me square in the eye and said, "You killed him." I gasped and had an inner panic attack, just as the man threw his head back in laughter, clearly thinking he just cracked the best joke in the world. Um sir, let me check my funny –o- meter. Yes, just as I expected … your joke sucked. Not funny.

A couple of minutes after the man was whisked away and the crowd returned to their seats, the band kicked back up and began playing "Sexy Back," and the dance floor filled back up with people ready to continue their night of getting down and dirty, fox trot style.

The End.

Okay, wait a second. You didn't really think I was going to end the book there, did you? Can we talk about this? I am feeling a little unsettled. A man just died in the middle of that beautiful party, and the night just carried on like nothing ever happened. He had probably worked way too hard his entire life to be invited to an event like that, to have the beach front mansion, the nice car and fancy clothes. Then, at the drop of a hat it was all over, and he was carried out to the hospital alone, with nobody next to him holding his hand.

Breaking news everybody: Money can't buy you eternal life. We are all going to croak, no matter how expensive our loafers are. And at that moment, it didn't matter how much money the man had made, who he had connections with, or how big his Manhattan apartment was. At that moment, the reality was he was being ushered out of a party on a stretcher, and the minute the door closed behind him everyone continued on as if he had just stepped outside for a cigarette. No matter how much money, power or fame that man had, nothing could buy his way out of his inevitable fate. His wealth was absolutely meaningless.

I was heartbroken. Working on this island, I have served people who have absolutely everything the world tells them they need or should have to be happy: the nice home, the beautiful wife, the small thighs and the flashy car. But these same people who "have it all" are by far some of the most miserable people I have ever met. Nothing they can purchase, wear, or do seems to fill that empty hole we ultimately all feel inside of us.

Someone please cue the tragic violin music. Bet you didn't see that serious rant coming. I'm full of surprises.

Eventually, the wine stopped being poured, the music died out, and the guests returned to their beachfront property. Kyle and I jumped back into our Toyota and drove back to our tiny, 400-square-foot apartment on the mainland, and I fell asleep with his arms around me, thanking God for the roof over my head and the people who love me, as I do every night. I may not have perfect hair or an article of clothing that costs more than $30, but I have God, I have love, and I have joy. At this moment of my existence, I am extremely wealthy.

The End.
For real this time.

About the Author

Katie Schnack is a writer and literary publicist based out of Austin, Texas. Born and raised in Minnesota, she now spends her days making fun of southern accents, eating queso and watching her husband act in plays. She thinks it is annoying when people mention their pets in their bio, but she doesn't know what else to include so... she has two cats.

For more information please visit katieschnack.com or send her a tweet at @katieschnack.

www.ingramcontent.com/pod-product-compliance
Lightning Source LLC
Chambersburg PA
CBHW051824040426
42447CB00006B/357